How Big is the Fly?
Asking the Right Questions

BONNIE JEAN SMITH

authorHOUSE®

AuthorHouse™
1663 Liberty Drive, Suite 200
Bloomington, IN 47403
www.authorhouse.com
Phone: 1-800-839-8640

First published by AuthorHouse 7/9/2007

ISBN: 978-1-4343-0522-0 (sc)

Printed in the United States of America
Bloomington, Indiana

This book is printed on acid-free paper.

Behavior: non-verbal communication, the act of imparting or interchanging thoughts, opinions, or information without the using words... (Wikipedia encyclopedia 2006)

Table of Contents

How Big is the Fly?

I knew my seven year old son, Ray, had peculiar behaviors when I saw him pointing to items he wanted instead of using words. Other peculiar behaviors I observed were these: he would go into hiding whenever a fly or a bee flew into the house or classroom and he would absolutely refuse to go outside whenever buzzing insects were flying about.

At school the educators explained to me Ray needed medication because he was showing some form of delusional, emotional behavioral disorder coupled with an anxiety mental illness. Yes, I could see it was true that when Ray drew pictures of flies and bees, they were always bigger than any other object in his drawings. His insects were exaggerated and looked more like meat eating dinosaurs than the small annoying insects they really are. In fact, the only time I remember Ray watching, not running, from flying insects was during a nature movie on flying insects where the camera always seemed to show close up pictures allowing viewers to see every minute detail. These insects happened to be eating, laying eggs and walking on an animal that was decaying. Not a pretty site! When the video emphasized the buzzing sound of the insects, Ray would cover his ears even though the volume of the television truly was not loud.

During the summer following his second grade, I found out why Ray was frightened of flies and bees. It was because he did not understand he was a giant, many times over, compared to these flying insects. I could tell he was truly terrified of them by his rapid breathing, breaking into a cold sweat, and wildly racing heart. These behaviors occurred every time one of the buzzing insects happened to be in the same area with Ray. At home I would have to hold and cover him with a small blanket until he was feeling safe. Many times we would also have to find and swat the invading insect or shoo it outside to freedom in order to ease his fears.

After countless attempts which were ineffective at trying to convince Ray how much bigger he was than tiny insects, I stumbled upon the information I needed to begin understanding and calming his fears. I finally asked my son the right question when I said, "How big is the fly?" He held up his small, trembling hands indicating the fly must be almost as large as a yardstick. At that moment, a paradigm shift occurred in the way I understood how my son concretely envisioned and communicated the world around him to others. Because I had asked the right question, I now understood how to interpret his behavior. Ray's answer made me understand that, from his point of view, a giant fly or bee might make its entrance at any moment to do lord knows what to him, perhaps eat him or lay eggs on him, like he had seen the insects do in the movie we had watched together. It was no wonder he looked at the rest of us as if we were nuts! When he showed me how large he believed the flying insects were, I began to wonder if Ray had a hearing problem of some sort. If he believed flying insects could be gigantic because of the ones we saw on the nature movie, could not also the sound of their buzzing been amplified for him and too loud for his ears even though the television seemed to be speaking at a normal volume for the rest of us? Instead of jumping to the school professionals' conclusion that Ray was delusional and had emotional anxiety behavioral disorders, I decided to have his hearing tested first, especially since there was not a history of mental illness in our family. Since I now realized how the close up shots made Ray believe these insects could actually be as large as a yardstick, could the insects he was hearing in his environment also be as loud to him as the camera enlarged insects in the video. A visit to the audiologist gave Ray a hearing diagnosis of hyperacusis (unusual sensitivity to specific sounds), meaning he heard *too* well. This was the reason those tiny insects were terrifying to him. Rather than putting him on the recommended psychotropic medication that would not have solved the problem, I bought him a pair of cool-looking earplugs. A big problem was solved with a simple solution. Ray started playing outside!

Ray was a very quiet child who played by himself. He neither fought nor was too loud, and yet, for the past two years, I had been receiving calls about his unwelcome behavior from the public schools. The first call I received was in regard to Ray following two boys in his first grade class who were walking around the classroom ignoring the teacher's request to stay in their seats. Not hearing the words spoken by the teacher, Ray noticed the boys. Thinking they were lining up to go somewhere, he got up out of his seat and joined them. These three boys were given referrals to the principal's office but Ray did not have a clue as to why he was in trouble.

In another incident happened the same day Ray received a suspension. He drew a picture of his first grade teacher for me at home. She had three heads and six arms flailing around. I was concerned about the way he had portrayed her. I returned Ray to school when his suspension was over and presented the disconcerting picture to his teacher. She paused momentarily and then said that that particular day was a very hard day for her and his drawing depicted exactly how she had felt. She thought it was wonderful the way Ray could draw what she was feeling. This teacher was professional enough to admit she had imperfect human days - days where a person wants to go back to bed and start over again because nothing is in sync. I liked her for that. I also liked the way she recognized and supported my son's strength in visual communication.

I found myself traveling more frequently to the public schools addressing the unwelcome behaviors of my children - behaviors that were nonexistent before their public school education began.

Unwelcome Behaviors

Once more, because of unwelcome behavior, I found myself driving from the city where I worked to the city where we lived in order to pick up one of my children at school. Sitting in rush hour traffic, I began to think about my family. I am a working "single mother"... one thing I never wanted to be! Carrying the stigma of *single mother* is not what I had planned for my life. I don't like the way most people's beliefs about single mothers tend to be on the negative side.

From my former marriage, I have four beautiful, loving children. I have a daughter, who is the oldest, and then three sons. All my children were raised with great manners. They are not rude; they are not loud or disrespectful. I did teach them, however, that they could respectfully disagree with anyone on this planet.

With the unwelcome school behaviors of two of my children, I have now entered a steep learning curve about the *whys* of behavior and do not depend entirely on a professional diagnosis. I learned quickly how too many professionals end up using Occam's razor or the simplest answer found within their professional silo to define unwelcome behavior. Not all professionals, but too many of them, tend *not* to look outside their own professionally isolated silo for evidence of an alternative, perhaps even a better root or underlying cause, for unwelcome behaviors that occur. I found myself looking at the entire picture for more practical reasons for unwelcome behaviors, looking not only at the child but also the child's environment and the family's culture. Perhaps my ability to reach and teach an individual child the skills needed to become an independent and self-determined person is the result of my years as an early childhood educator, exposure to world cultures, and the fact I have many siblings. I have learned from all my experiences. How many two year olds can walk up to someone and say they have an auditory processing problem and need time to process a directive? How many young children can say they are sensory over-stimulated, hence explaining that is the reason they are having a migraine? How many crying babies can tell a caring adult they are crying just because they want to hear their own voice? Children sometimes use unwelcome behavior to communicate to adults that something about either their bodies or their environment is not working correctly. It is our job as loving parents and guardians to figure out what that something is that needs to be altered. Regrettably, the current trend seems to criminalize school children's behaviors rather than analyzing it in order to find its function or purpose. Children, for the most part, are neither deviant nor mini adults.

With all that said, today's phone call was not about my son, Ray, who was currently in third grade. This time it was about my first grade son, Moogie! Sitting in rush hour traffic, I mulled over the phone call about my son and his fourth behavioral incident at school. This time it was not a social worker from the school who called but my daughter DeeDee, an eighth grader, who was frantically telling me Moogie had held himself hostage in the school for four and one half hours. School personnel would not let her go to him. Crying, she said she knew Moogie was very scared. She explained to me how the building principal had threatened her with suspension if she did not get on the school bus and go home without her six-year-old brother. DeeDee would not get on the bus. After delivering one last threat to her, the building principal turned around and walked back into the school. DeeDee did not want to leave her baby brother. She was terrified the school bus would leave without her and terrified to leave Moogie so she sat on the curb with her mind racing, trying to think. The understanding bus driver told DeeDee not to worry. He offered to wait as long as she needed to make up her mind as to what she was going to do. DeeDee finally decided to get on the bus, go to the daycare center, and call Mom - me.

Getting calls from the school about Moogie was not strange. The calls were never anything major on his behalf. At least that was my belief. Moogie weighed forty pounds. He was full of energy, fun, empathy, wonder and life. The very first call I received had been while he was in kindergarten. When I arrived at the school, I found Moogie sitting in the coatroom, spitting and crying. He would not talk to me. I took him immediately to our clinic to find out if he was having an asthma attack. The doctor thought it was amazing Moogie could suck the phlegm like liquid out of his airways even though he was spitting it out on the floor. That was why he did not speak to me. He was trying to breathe. I did not look upon this incident as Moogie being a behavior problem.

Since kindergarten, Moogie has had the medical diagnoses of asthma and ADHD (Attention Deficit Hyperactivity Disorder), an impulsive type, whatever all that meant. I did not want to put him on ADHD medication as the school had suggested. Too many serious side effects in my opinion! After all, I was not having any of the problematic behaviors with my son at home that they were telling me were unmanageable in school.

Ok! Ok! I did finally decide to put Moogie on medication in kindergarten. Why did I even reconsider the psychotropic medication? It was due to the fact that Moogie's second school incident of unwelcome behavior also occurred in kindergarten when he carried his two dollar allowance to school one day. I watched him tuck it safely into his front pocket. I never thought about the fact that there was a golden arches fast food restaurant across the street from his school. Moogie took it upon himself to leave the kindergarten classroom to cross a very busy avenue to buy french fries that day. His teacher did not know Moogie was missing from her class. The blaring horns of semi-trucks caught the attention of the front office secretaries and they alerted the proper staff to retrieve my son.

My children attended a large daycare center for years and they were never once reported for dangerous behavior problems - not the kind the school was describing to me.

If I had lost my child as this school had, I would face an open child protection case. If the daycare had lost my child, they would either loose their license or be fined. However, in this case at hand, the school punished and suspended my son for leaving school property. It was *his* problem, not *their* responsibility.

The french fry incident took place during the same year Moogie unbuckled his seatbelt, opened the door, and walked out of our moving car every time we passed a motorcycle he wanted to see. His impulsivity in both instances could have killed him. It was then I put him on medication and also made him promise me he would never leave the school building, a classroom, *or* a car again without adult permission.

Moogie's second school incident of unwelcome behavior in kindergarten also resulted in a suspension. The music teacher wrote on the suspension form that Moogie had exposed his private parts to the class and urinated in her trash can. When I asked Moogie what had occurred, he explained how his class had been singing for a few minutes when he realized he needed to use the restroom. He raised his hand and asked permission to go. The teacher told him no, telling him he should have gone when the class stopped on the way down to music class. He would just have to wait another twenty minutes for class to end. Moogie told me he did not have to use the bathroom when the class went as a group. Remembering his promise to me to obey the teachers, Moogie was now caught between his promise and his innate need. Resolving this dilemma, he went into the music teacher's office and placed her trash can behind her desk. With his back to the door and the light turned off, he urinated in her trash can because he could not wait another twenty minutes. I refused to sign the first, second, third, fourth and fifth form the school sent home to me. Finally I received an incident report that stated: "Student had to use the restroom after music class had begun. The student asked to go to the restroom; instructed to wait until the end of class. The student went into the music teacher's office and with his back to the door and the light turned off, urinated in her trash can. Some of the students heard the sound and laughed. Student suspended one day." I signed this form. What was so hard about writing the truth? Why criminalize children instead of saying the student had to use the restroom and the teacher did not deem it necessary? The school had tried to make him a sexual deviant, which is an extremely serious charge. How many students are "over-identified" as to having mental health and/or behavioral problems because professionals are having an impatient human moment? How many families are put through hell because of it?

Today's phone call from my daughter, made me question how a happy, loving, forty pound, extremely impulsive, medicated first grader can hold himself hostage for four and a half hours while out-maneuvering the professionals at a public school, including his one-on-one paraprofessional? Why didn't they distract my son by changing his focus and talking about things he loved...like Batman's car, motorcycles and video games. That is how I easily redirect him. Didn't the school professionals read anything I gave them from the evaluation I had had done for my son at the University's Pediatric Neuropsychiatry Clinic? No, of course not! I am a single parent; they are professionals. Until this day I had been a single parent wearing rose-colored glasses. Well, it took long enough for me to wake up! The professionals were looking for preconceived concepts in which they could fit Moogie's behaviors and not actually looking at the environment where the behavior occurred. They should have asked questions like what happened right before the behavior and what did my son gain as a consequence for his behavior?

I pulled up into the parking lot where there were only a few cars and walked into a darkened, foreboding school building. As I headed toward the social worker's office, the empty halls echoed with the wailing sound of a lost soul. It was my son. Oh my, God! The sound was like nothing I had ever heard before in my entire life. It was a painful wailing sound of despair and misery ... the sound that would make loving parents run through a burning building to save their child. I ran down the hallway reaching the social worker's office only to find the door closed and blocked by the social worker standing in front of it, trying to tell me all that had transpired. I started to push past her to reach my son when she told me they had called the police on my baby. Pausing only briefly, I remember asking her why they would involve and threaten him by calling the police. My son loved police officers. Not waiting for an answer from her, I sprang into the office and found it in shambles. Two huge wooden tables were overturned and every chair in the room had the seats and the backs of them cut into pieces. The large window shades were torn and hanging down.

I found my son standing inside what looked to be like some kind of duct work for air in the room. Only his tiny legs were visible from the knees down with his little white socks, one up and one rolled down over the top of his black, hard-soled leather shoes. His pants were torn exposing his skin that was covered with what appeared to be green and orange circles. I knelt down on my knees, calling him repeatedly, until he bent down to look at me. I saw the same green and orange circles covering a chocolate brown face and his huge dark brown, worried eyes. He crawled quickly out to me. I sat all the way down, crossing my legs, cradling and rocking him. I remember telling him repeatedly how I would never leave him unless God took me away from him. He finally slumped into my lap. His howling and weeping stopped. The social worker had been speaking to me…, "blah, blah, blah". I could not tell you what she said. I held my baby. At some point, she eventually left the room. I picked Moogie up and walked out of the building with only the janitor to see us out.

How could this happen to my child? To any child? Treated like a wild animal, not like a human being. I had believed school personnel were "the professionals". I thought they knew how to work with *all* children. At least that is what they told me about themselves.

When we arrived home, DeeDee held her brother, crying and telling him she was sorry she could not get to him to help him. We all sat and wept holding each other. I fixed dinner but everyone just picked over the food on their plates. We couldn't eat.

Disrespectful, Disobedient, Disruptive, and Dangerous

After bathing Moogie and putting him into bed, I talked with him, assuring him he was safe. In our conversation, from his point of view, he let me know what had occurred in school that day. Moogie and his one-on-one paraprofessional (para) were leaving the electronic reading library. His reading teacher explained to him that he would be going to music class next. Moogie loved music class, especially today when he would be demonstrating his tap dancing talent. (After all, he had won the Sammy Davis Jr. Tap Dancing Award from the American Variety Theatre Company.) However, instead of taking him to music class as she was supposed to do, the para, deciding she was interested in looking at some of the electronic library books herself, took Moogie back into the library. By doing this, the transitioning process the reading teacher had just helped my son understand was broken and made him think it was time to pick out another book to read on the computer. When the para was finished perusing her electronic book selection, she said it was time to go to music class now, but my son insisted it was time to go back to reading. The para threatened him stating if he did not go to music right this moment she would take away his tap shoes. Moogie responded by telling her she was from "Hell, from down not from up because she was a thief and a liar". This blunt, learned-in-Sunday school accusation, made the para angry. Her next course of action was to threaten him with a trip to the principal's office if he continued to be *disrespectful*. Thus, a line had been drawn in the sand. Which one of them had the power and would control this situation? Moogie lay down on the floor and would not move, now becoming *disobedient and defiant*. The para grabbed his little arm and literally dragged him down the hallways to the social worker's office who spoke kind and reassuring words to my son. With that, he got up and went back to his classroom. When the class returned from music, however, my son told me the teacher and the para began arguing in front of him and the entire class about who was supposed to help him with his work. This upset Moogie so much that he began crying and tearing up his work sheets. Since he was now being "destructive", the teacher rushed over to him while still arguing with the para. She grabbed him by his arms so he kicked her with his hard leather soled shoe. This made him "*dangerous*". The teacher then took all the children out of the classroom because his crying was *disruptive* to the education of the other students. Moogie told me the teacher and his paraprofessional were acting crazy, yelling at each other. It scared him and made him think he was a bad boy and had caused the fighting between the adults. He wanted to come home because he said school was not a good place to go.

The para dragged Moogie down the hallway once again. This time Moogie, who lay on the floor as limp as a rag doll, was dragged into the social worker's office during student passing time. Once inside the room, Moogie immediately stood up. Going over to the social worker's desk and picking up a pair of scissors, he began cutting paper. He told me one of the teachers told him to put the scissors down because he could poke out his eyes. Given this novel idea, he decided they would let him come home if he threatened to hurt his eyes. (He told me he would never hurt his eyes because he only had two!) School staff were now afraid because he had picked up the scissors. They had warned him of the dangers and were unsure of what to do next. Moogie thought these people were silly because everyone knew scissors could not jump up by themselves and hurt your eyes. You had to run with them to get hurt. Moogie also knew he had gained the power and was in control of the situation. The staff went into action by closing him in the room by himself and would not let him out. They did not let him call me or contact his 13-year-old sister to come downstairs to help him. Sister found out his situation from other students who knew her.

Moogie told me he was very, very scared. He told me he became invisible. I asked him how he knew he was invisible and he replied because whenever any adult came into the room, they did not see him anymore. I understood, from an adult's perspective, that everyone was either ignoring him in hopes it would make his behavior stop or they were busy trying to figure out what to do with him. My son told me a police officer came into the room and that made him feel happy and safe. He ran to the officer and the officer picked him up. Moogie told me, while the officer was holding him, he fussed at the school staff telling them my son was a baby. (I'm sure he was wondering why all these adults could not handle this one small child!) My son asked if the officer would give him a ride home but the officer said I would have to come get him. Moogie loved police officers. He loved them so much he would call 9-1-1 and wait on the front stoop of our house with milk and cookies to give the officer who responded to his call. I held Moogie in my arms that night until he fell asleep.

I received a paper from the school social worker that stated Moogie was suspended for 14 consecutive days for being *disrespectful, disobedient, disruptive, and dangerous* and I needed to attend a manifestation meeting about the hostage incident that had occurred. I was angry. More importantly, I did not know what our rights were. My son had held himself hostage. On top of that, what was a manifestation meeting anyway?

After everyone was in bed and asleep that night, I thought about how I could build credibility and not be looked down upon as an ignorant, single mother. I had to find what I needed to do to protect my children.

Reading is fundamental for education. I found there is a lot of money available for professionals to do research to prove how most problems that occur with children point to single parents. I have heard from some educators that single parents do not know how to raise their children. Many of them cited research they had read. My perception is this: if you look hard enough, you can find data to back almost any point of view. In my opinion, there are too many research grants showing how single parents are a liability to our society and are a potential danger to every child, especially the disabled child.

Single Parent

I know from first hand experience that being a "single parent" is not an easy seat to sit on while having to prove credibility to professionals. Professional researchers, who are still arguing the old "Nature vs. Nurture" data, have shown how the original researchers deliberately skewed the information that had been collected. They wanted to prove they were more professional then the next professional. They tried to prove two parent families are better, healthier and so forth than single families. However, they ignored data on serial killers, murders, and school shooters that have come out of two parent and economically stable homes.

My ex-husband Gary, father of all four of my children, was abusive: emotionally, monetarily and physically. I asked myself, "If he treated me the way he does now when I first met him, would I have even gone out with him?" My answer was, no! It had been a negative process that inched my self-esteem away, little by little, year after year, until mentally we were living inside a cycle of abusive domestic violence with little hope. I had to find a way out of this cycle of abuse for my children and myself. I did! We made it out when I was seven months pregnant with my youngest child.

As a single parent family, my children and I had survived domestic violence and were returning to peace and structure in our home. When I say structure, I mean we had meat loaf on Monday nights and movies on Friday nights. I came from a military family. My daughter DeeDee, out of all of my children, bonded with her father. While I was in the military, her father took care of her from the time she was born until she turned five years old. When he abandoned us completely, she was thirteen years old and then had to get to know *my* rules which were very different from his. Her father never saw

DeeDee perform in any of her English hand bell performances, dance recitals, plays at the theatre, or her sixth grade, eighth grade, and high school graduations, even though he promised her every time that he would be there. He missed a beautiful, talented performer. He now reappears on our doorstep, sometimes every other year, making and breaking promises uttered to our children. It has not been trouble-free raising four different people but I am grateful he left and did not bring the chaos he chose for his life into our lives.

Out of this marriage I learned how to survive domestic violence and all of its facets including how it affects families, specifically women and children. I became an employed, educated expert on the subject of domestic violence and, as a woman's advocate, became a community trainer based out of the first battered women's shelter in the nation. I worked with children and their mothers. Many times I would be there when they realized for the first time that they were safe. I could see the fear and mistrust in their eyes slowly dissipate. Consistency and structure made all the difference in the world for these hurt families who had just come off a roller coaster ride continually living from crisis to crisis. These mothers complained to me about the unwelcome behaviors of their children after they came to the shelter. Many mothers thought their children had gone insane. I would explain to them that these behaviors were due to the fact that their children now felt safe and could let out all their anger and fear that they had had to keep secret inside of them, feeling helpless while living with their abuser.

Lead poisoning and Autism

My two oldest sons, Ray and Moogie, had gotten lead poisoning at the ages of five months and two years old. The lead was removed from inside their bodies by taking chelating medication that smelled like skunk. The only way I could get them to take it was to hide the capsule granules under a teaspoon of catsup. Why use catsup? Well, my thoughts were this: since tomato paste stops the smell of skunk and catsup is made from tomatoes, catsup would mask the smell of the skunk medication. It worked!

Doctors had different ideas about the effects of lead poisoning. Some stated there were no symptoms; others said there were many symptoms. At least they could all agree on this one point: lead poisoning was bad. Just how bad was it? During that time, lead poisoning research was new and no professional would say.

I observed very unusual developmentally delayed behaviors in my sons. Moogie, at five months old, was crawling and playing "vroom-vroom" with plastic trucks. Ray, at the age of two, would only eat two tablespoons of macaroni and cheese, taco flavored chips and apple juice and nothing else. The doctors said I was worrying too much about my sons and told me they would both grow out of my concerns. We had nurses who would come to visit us in our home for my two year old child because of the lead poisoning. I welcomed the adult company but I did not treat either of my sons any differently than I did my seven year old daughter when she was their age.

In third grade my oldest son, Ray, went through a special education evaluation by the public school because of unwelcome behavior concerns that were presented to me by them. Ray was always a very quiet child. He started talking at the age of 13 months but stopped talking and eating when he was two years old. He did not start talking again until he turned four but this time he was using fewer words and pointing when he wanted something. Ray did not make a fuss at home and never caused any problems in school until his third grade class began studying the Amazon Rain Forest. The class decorated their room until it really had the look and feel of a rain forest - very busy and rich in colors. Ray began his unwelcome school behaviors by walking to the back of the classroom everyday and tipping over a chair with one finger. When the teacher asked him to pick up the chair, he would shake his head, no. His teacher would then send him to the social worker's office where the walls were stark white and had nothing hanging on them. Ray would go in, dim the lights, climb up onto the social worker's lap, and rock.

I would, of course, come pick him up and take him to daycare where he functioned just fine. After his school evaluation, Ray had the educational criteria of autism. What was AUTISM? Hell, if I knew! I believed the school professionals understood what it meant and they would take care of it at school. They took care of it by deciding to move Ray to a different elementary school where they had professionals who understood autism. I wanted Ray to change schools but not for the same reason. When Moogie was a kindergartener and began attending the same school as his older brother, he would leave his own classroom and get Ray out of his second grade classroom whenever he had problems, such as another child taking a toy away from him. Moogie would then return with his brother who would take back the plundered toy from the other child. I received many calls from the school about Ray, the "righter of all toy wrongs", coming to the aid of his younger brother, Moogie. Ray would fuss at the child who had taken the toy away from Moogie, return the toy to him, hug his brother and then depart back to his own classroom. The kindergarten teacher stated he did not understand their conversations because Ray and Moogie spoke their own language. I knew they had their own language. It had concerned me but their pediatrician assured me not to be alarmed.

To get a referral for a comprehensive evaluation from our pediatrician, I had to demonstrate that Ray did not understand the English language. Using jibber jabber, I smiled at Ray in front of the doctor in the clinic examination room and pointed to a cup of water I had set on the desk. Ray looked at me cautiously and then walked slowly over to the desk while keeping eye contact with my face. I smiled at him as he picked up the cup of water and quickly handed it to me. He smiled back at me and returned to the bin of toys in the room to continue playing. After using pretend language to communicate with Ray, the doctor agreed we needed a specialist to look at his ears and check his speech. As it turned out, Ray had water in his ears. There was no infection, just water. He could hear sounds but no clear sounds as in the words used in speech. He took medication to dry up the water in his ears. However, by this time Ray had missed many of the basic sounds that are building blocks most toddlers are able to hear to practice for speech.

I saw my children at home and at their daycare with strengths and unique needs just like any other "regular" children. Only in school did they have unwelcome behaviors. I had to complain in order to get speech support for Ray in the public schools. Because of that, I was labeled an overly concerned, single parent and yet, he and his brother had both received private speech support in a daycare setting and were given a recommendation to acquire continued speech services at school! At first, the school informed me my son did not qualify for school speech services, even though they had performed no tests to come to that conclusion. At that time, I did not know schools were required to evaluate my sons at my request. After I told the school social worker what the pediatrician had recommended, she informed me that she had made the suggestion for an evaluation and now assured me an assessment would be done.

On one of the academic tests performed, I sat in the room with the evaluator and saw how she gave Ray a hint to the question she was asking so, of course, Ray would guess the right answer she was looking for. It appeared this person was in a hurry and had to be at another school site in less than an hour. Since Ray had been rushed through her part of the evaluation and she had helped him along the way by giving him answers, I complained, in writing, about the process that I had witnessed. Ray magically qualified for speech services!

Gavin was born

Gavin, my youngest son, was born in a joyous, carnival atmosphere. My children were waiting for this birth outside of the delivery room in a nearby area of the hospital with my girlfriends' children. I very much appreciated the support I had from friends since this was my only child born without their father being present. The youngest woman, Sandy, who was there to support me was also a co-worker of mine. She honestly asked the doctor and the nurses present in the delivery room where the "tearing sheets" were located. Everyone in the room turned their attention to her. Sandy proceeded to explain how she had seen a movie where the woman was given sheets to hold on to so she could tear them during the birth process. The room fell silent until one of the nurses walked over to a lower cabinet and showed Sandy where they kept the "tearing sheets". Then the mothers in the room erupted in gleeful laughter.

Shortly afterwards, I had the experience of taking a long, entertaining walk through the halls of the hospital with Sandy following behind me carrying a folded sheet in order to catch the baby if it decided to fall out of my womb "because I was walking"! We returned to the delivery room and I lay on the birthing bed looking up at the faces of all of my friends there to support me and my family. I finally gave a very loud gurgling yell during the final push. Gavin was born! He was a very alert child. In fact, as the doctor readied to cut the umbilical cord, Gavin grabbed the scissors and pulled them to his face to get a better look at the shiny object. The doctors and nurses were amazed. It took five minutes to safely remove his tiny hand grasped around the cutting instrument. Gavin just kept staring at them. He was not even a minute old, but filled with curiosity. Wrapped in a small blanket, Gavin lay at my side. My girlfriends, their children, and my children paraded back into the delivery room to look at their new Godchild, friend and sibling. Moogie's face was shining happily with amazement. He asked me how I got his baby brother "out my mouth" since he had heard me yell Gavin out of my stomach! Moogie's comment caused a ripple of laughter in the room. From that moment on, every night before prayers, Moogie would sing, "The Ritzy, Bitsy Spider" instead of "itsy bitsy spider" to his new brother.

Understanding Processes

The morning after Moogie's four and a half hour, self-hostage, first grade school incident, I woke everyone up, got ready and took my children to daycare. I tried to keep our routine as close to the normal structure as possible because I did not want to show the fear and stress I was holding inside. Explaining to the staff at the daycare center what had occurred at school, they were very supportive. They helped me gather information about Moogie from all of the daycare teachers who knew him. Even the volunteer grandmothers gathered him under their wings and told me that the school must not know anything about children to think Moogie was anything but a wonderful, loving child.

Feeling much better, knowing other adults saw what I did in my child, I took the information and went home. I watched the President of the United States on television giving a speech about America's most precious resource, "our children". That night I made up my mind to call the White House to let them know what was happening in our school district to "our most precious resource".

A woman named Rose answered the telephone when I called. She listened as I recanted, with bouts of weeping and anger, the horror my son had experienced. When I finished, she asked me to wait a moment. Then she came back to me with the telephone number of a parent advocacy organization located in my city. After thanking her, I called the suggested organization and gave them the name of an advocate with whom I wanted to speak. I left a message on her answering machine. Once again I called and tried to get help. This time I finally broke down in tears telling my story to a wonderful receptionist who offered to mail me a packet of information. This eye-opening information showed me there was much more I needed

20

to know about the laws and our rights. I learned there was a legal process in place to help us. I had never heard any information about this process before. Was the school aware of it? How many parents knew about it? I remembered reading an Individualized Education Plan (IEP) for both of my sons. I had read the documents and pulled off the attached procedural safeguards and threw them away without even looking at them as though it was an advertisement flier inside of a bill. Little did I know it had quite a lot of information pertaining to our educational rights. It included lists of organizations in charge of teaching parents about special education rights. It mentioned state offices I could contact if I disagreed with any part of the educational plan the school might want to implement for my sons.

Feverishly I began to read any information I could find pertaining to schools and special education. I found out there were federal and state laws, rules and regulations, that protected the rights of children with disabilities and also gave parents the right to have a say in their child's special education process from beginning to end. I found out the school was supposed to educate me and include me in this process. They were not to write educational plans to help my child, under the pretense that their decisions had been made out of the goodness of their hearts, and then have me sign off showing I agreed with what they had done. I was "supposed" to give them *informed* consent. In other words, I was supposed to understand *what* I was signing and *why* I was signing all the IEPs.

I found out there were hundreds of pages and I read each one. I called the State Department of Education with a complaint of what had occurred. They spoke to me about a Free and Appropriate Education (FAPE) and the Least Restrictive Environment (LRE). In his entire life, I knew my son had never behaved in any other place as they stated he had behaved in school that day. The complaint investigator told me that if my son did not have unwanted behaviors in the community or at home, then Emotional Behavior Disorder (EBD) educational criteria "should not be considered" under state and federal criteria. The complaint investigator sent the law to me that explained the Minnesota criteria for EBD and autism.

A Manifestation Determination Meeting

I arrived for the manifestation meeting and waited for one of the daycare teachers who was coming to talk about Moogie and defend his character. As I waited in the social worker's office alone, the principal entered the room and asked me to put it in writing that I would not bring Moogie back to this school. She said if I wrote, signed, and dated the paper, she would not call the police to press charges against my baby for the destruction of school property he had caused. They claimed he used the scissors to cut up all of the leather chairs in the office, flipped over two huge wooden tables, and destroyed the shades on the twenty-foot high windows in the room. Darn it! I did it again! I signed papers under the duress and fear of trying to protect my baby without the understanding of what I was signing. Not until the evening after this meeting would I thoroughly read the occupational therapy report again and find out that my son did not have the fine motor strength to do what they claimed he had done in this room.

The manifestation meeting started. For my support, I had the school district's only parent advocate who was an African-American woman, and one of Moogie's daycare teachers. The school had what seemed to be twenty people even though, in reality, there were only twelve. At first I felt very uneasy. These were educational professionals. My uneasiness left, however, as the conversation turned to Moogie and I heard others say how unskilled and far behind he was from his peers; how he needed to be at a segregated site and in a small class size with more adults in order to help *explosive* children like him. With righteous anger, I waited patiently until the psychologist and the classroom teacher finished painting their dismal picture of Moogie. When they had finished their speech of the "He will never" and making a list of everything that Moogie would never be able to accomplish in his life, the social worker, too, tried to convince me that my son should go to this special, segregated school that was noted for students with emotional or behavior problems. I immediately said no to this suggestion. The social worker continued to explain how the first grade teacher and the principal both thought it best because my son was not, and could not, learn up to the same speed as the "regular" children. His classroom teacher reiterated the fact that Moogie did not know his colors or his alphabet. I listened carefully and wondered what kind of school I had enrolled my children. All my children knew their colors and their letters. I read to them every night, at least four nights a week, from what my children called chapter books. In fact, I kept a dated record of all of their work, milestones, and accomplishments, such as the first time they wrote their names. I came from a family where we played school. Learning was fun. This carried over when I had my own children. I also had evaluations of all my children's academic baselines from the daycare center they attended. I opened my file box and pulled out all of the data containing Moogie's educational baselines. The data showed me his teacher had no idea what he knew and what he understood. Moogie knew how to read and write. He knew math facts that, at this time, the schools were not yet teaching in first grade. The daycare teacher stated how she saw Moogie as a very intelligent, caring, and compassionate student. She showed staff the baselines for him in her classroom, which totally contradicted the schools data. I brought out the University's Pediatric Neuropsychological Clinic report and read the summary to the team showing how this evaluation also contradicted the school's information about Moogie. I presented scores from another community psychologist which were much higher than the scores the school psychologist had given him. I had a current letter from a doctor at the University's Pediatric Neuropsychiatry Clinic who had tested Moogie which stated that my son was so bright he might get on someone's last nerve but he was *not* emotionally or behaviorally disabled. All these reports seemed to make the school staff back down about the emotional behavior and disabled placement for him. Instead, they suggested my son go into the Citywide Autism Program, the same as my oldest son. It was then that I brought out all of the weekly work Moogie had been doing at the daycare center for the past six months. I passed these items around the table along with photographs of him doing every day first grade things at home, in the community, and at daycare. There were stories he had written and books he had made about numbers, colors, insects and leaves. There was even a Red Cross book he had put together using spelling words like "bandage". These were all materials my son had written!

I told these people the school did not know how to teach him. I told them he was a very polite, loving, and caring child. The daycare teacher told them Moogie was in a class of 27 children and he functioned very well, knew all of the rules and followed them. She told them he had never been a behavior problem while in the daycare or on field trips. She ended by saying that perhaps no one at school was listening to him.

A Time to Learn

What was the outcome of my son's manifestation and placement meeting today?

Moogie would go to the same school as his older brother, Ray, and become part of the Citywide Autism Program. I still did not know what autism was when I left that meeting but I would not give anyone sitting around the table that information. I agreed to the new regular education placement with one-on-one adult support. Another placement meeting would have to take place at the new school. This gave me little time to learn as much as I could about Autism Spectrum Disorders.

After this meeting, the principal implied I had won this "round" for my son because the school district was not going to send Moogie to a separate institutional site. What did this mean? I thought the schools were there to help, nurture and educate *all* children; I did not like the implication that there was a battle for my son's right to be educated. How many other parents had gone through this battle with the schools and lost? How many more parents are still battling the schools not knowing they have rights? I knew I had to share what I was learning with other parents anytime and anywhere possible.

Teaching

Now I had a new purpose to learn about our rights, the school system, and about disabilities. I began attending many conferences learning about all disabilities, including Emotional Behavioral Disorders (EBD) and Attention Deficit Hyperactive Disorder (ADHD). I studied what mechanisms doctors' believe caused these disabilities. I read as much as I could find on autism and developmental disabilities.

Assuming I would receive support from my church, I was disappointed when I eventually realized my pastors did not believe in ADHD - at least not what I had taught them. They invited two men from a well known church social service agency to come to one of our member meetings and educate interested parishioners about this disability. As we sat around the table, the men began explaining what happens in the mind of a person with ADHD. Sometimes they could not remember a definition or a process and I would help them. Finally, one of the men said to our group that he did not understand why the church had asked them to come to explain ADHD since it was apparent I knew more about the disability than they did. I realized at that moment I was still living in the "single mother" realm, meaning how could I actually know much about anything! I was a single mother after all who did not even know how to keep a good man as the head of household and so was now fighting poverty.

Knowing Our Rights

The day came for Moogie's meeting for placement at his new school. I arrived early and had made notes for myself, including *not* to sign anything at the school but rather take the information home and read over it for understanding and accuracy.

I liked Moogie's new one-on-one paraprofessional who happened to be an autism teacher - finally someone who understood autistic behavior vs. emotional behavior. More importantly, she understood all of the data given to her, including what I had shared about my son. This para/teacher invited the heads of all the departments in the school building including janitors, media center, cafeteria, nurse, social worker and principal to Moogie's special education placement meeting. She gave my son a tag of "code green" which meant that if anything went wrong with his behavior, an announcement of a "code green" would be made. At that time staff were to move all students out of the hallways and into their classrooms or work areas. Not because Moogie was dangerous but to protect his anonymity and keep him from being shamed in front of others. When I asked the teacher why she was expecting wrong behaviors, she explained how Moogie had been rewarded for his misbehaviors at his previous school - suspension meant he was sent home and to his daycare, which is exactly where he wanted to be. His wrong behaviors had been reinforced and he was given the tools to get what he wanted. Since he had been given power and control at that school, it would only be natural for him to try to establish that same power and control here. The objective of the new plan was to teach Moogie that misbehaviors in school would not result in him being sent home. We needed him to want to stay in school and not be afraid as well as eliminate negative behaviors. The autism teacher knew Moogie did not trust schools. For that reason, she was not only expecting wrong behaviors from him, she expected his behaviors to escalate with the hope of this school sending him home like his last school had done. After all, Moogie believed he was a bad boy and that schools did not like him. They had wanted a police officer to hurt him. I knew she was correct. His anxiety level was very high at home the closer it came time for him to go to school.

The day arrived when Moogie was supposed to go to school. I asked his one-on-one teacher if she wanted me to park outside the school. She said no. If he asked to call me then he would recognize the difference between calling me on my cell phone number or at my job. I waited anxiously by my phone at work, waiting for a call that Moogie had run away from school trying to get home. Finally, the anticipated call came around 10:00 AM. The teacher was on the phone laughing. I asked her if my son was all right. She replied he was fine and that he was in his classroom with the other students. She then told me the sequence of events that took place that morning.

When Moogie arrived at school, she was outside standing at the bus waiting to greet him. They walked into the school and into his new classroom together. The students all welcomed him and gave him cards they had made for him. After school announcements, the classroom teacher passed out worksheets. When Moogie received his worksheet, he crossed his little arms high on his chest. The autism teacher told him it was time to work and he told her he was not going to work. She then told him they needed to go to the quiet room until he was ready to work. She understood he was very scared. They left the classroom and started down the hall. Moogie stopped and stripped off all of his clothes, including shoes and socks. He began streaking down the hallway. The autism teacher took out her walkie-talkie and announced, "Code Green". The staff at the school did what was in the prearranged plan. Janitors went to the doors and pretended to be fixing or wiping windows. Moogie ran past one janitor and was greeted nonchalantly by him as though he wasn't running down the hallway naked! The second janitor opened the outside door, which was a wise thing to do. You see, it was March and there was still quite a lot of snow on the ground and the wind was gusting. The autism teacher did not chase Moogie; she stood by his pile of clothes, waiting. When no one chased him and no one told him he was a bad boy, he turned around on his own and came back. The autism teacher said she wished she had a camera as she watched a little frozen fudgesickle come down the hall shivering. Moogie walked to his clothes and put them on saying , "Ok, let's go work". That was the end of his *defiant, disrespectful, disruptive, and dangerous* unwanted behaviors in school. All of these behaviors were diminished without labeling my son as a flasher, without giving him a ticket from the police liaison officer which, in turn, would have resulted in dragging our family into the county's juvenile justice system. Moogie taught me about the function of behaviors and how to look at:

A. the Antecedent, what happened before the behavior

B. the Behavior that is unwelcome at school and

C. the Consequence of the student getting what they wanted.

Many professionals call this strength of students "manipulating behaviors" but this was not a planned and well-thought-out behavior. I wonder if they would label a three month old as manipulative when they cry just because they want to communicate? It would be much more productive to teach a child who uses unwelcome behaviors how to get what they need in their environment by using a more acceptable course of action.

Changes

After three great years at Moogie's new school, different unwelcome behaviors started. These behaviors were in the form of running away from school or school avoidance. Moogie was quite good at running away. He never made a fuss if his anxiety rose; he just waited for the adult that was supposed to be his support to turn their head and then he would disappear. Moogie was often trying to come home where he felt safe. No one ever seemed to understand why he would leave the school but he always talked to his family about it.

The first incident Moogie told me about was when his new case manager wanted him to leave his class work and come with him - leave work he had been told by his classroom teacher to finish. Moogie, being a very concrete person, said he could not come until he finished what his teacher had asked him to do. The new case manager, wearing an angry face, told Moogie to come or he would let the other children know he was not following directions. Feeling anxious, but not wanting to be shamed or be a bad boy, Moogie got up and ran into the boys' bathroom where he started to cry. The case manager followed him into the bathroom and told him to stop crying or he would bring the whole class in to watch him. Moogie kept crying and started bouncing his back on a toilet stall sidewall. (Mind you, this new male case manager and teacher had visited us in our home. I always invited teachers to come so they could observe my children in their home environment, hoping to give the educators clues as to how to teach and reach my children in a positive way.)

That was a day I received a call from his case manager informing me I had to pick Moogie up from school because he was suspended. He told me the principal was considering calling the police to report that Moogie had destroyed school property. A toilet stall wall had dropped under the force of Moogie's back bouncing on and off of it.

Remembering the threats of using the police against us that we had received at Moogie's previous school, I told the case manager I would sue the school if they called the police. I also told him I would bring a "damn screwdriver" and put the wall back up myself with Moogie's help. When I arrived, I found no one had called the police so I brought my son home with me. A janitor had already put the wall back in place.

The atmosphere in the school had changed that year with the installation of another new principal. Staff seemed to be under unusual duress, not from the students but from the school district.

At this time my son, Ray, had a very good teacher and was in one of the most inclusive classrooms I have ever observed. This fifth grade teacher would teach a lesson for ten minutes and then calmly say, "Everybody Hands!" at which all the students would raise one or both of their hands. Then he would say, "Move". Most of the class would clap their hands. Those students who did not clap, kept their hands held high in the air indicating they needed more help to understand the lesson. It was amazing to watch. Every student who clapped their hands moved over to a student closest to them who did not clap and would re-teach the lesson to them. It was wonderful watching an inclusive village at work.

Moogie had a new paraprofessional during his fourth grade year. In fact, he shared her with another student who apparently received more attention than Moogie. Moogie did not mind. He said Randy was a nice kid and it was wonderful how the para worked with Randy because it reminded Moogie of him and me working together. The para was nice to Moogie, too, but she worked more with Randy. At this time, I did not depend on schools to educate my children any more. I taught them basic reading, writing and arithmetic at home. The district administrators complained about not enough money to pay teachers' salaries and the teachers never knew if they were going to have a job or not the following year. Teaching was very stressful in our district and it did not matter whether you were a new or a seasoned teacher. In other words, I learned teachers are human beings too, not just "professionals".

Partners

It was unbelievable when a parent advocate at the school district office told me about a leadership training program sponsored by the Minnesota Governor's Council for People with Developmental Disabilities, called Partners in Policymaking® (Partners 2007). I applied and was accepted into this program. Through it, I became aware of processes that I did not know existed for persons with disabilities. This training was reported to be a Best Practice training to help persons with developmental disabilities and their families. I attended sessions once a month for eight months - 128 hours with top of the line training that was free for parents of children with developmental disabilities and adults with developmental disabilities. In the training, each participant needed to work on a project of their choice. My project was to help students with Emotional Behavior Disorders work their way out of an emotional behavior program. Learning their strengths and unique needs, and using them, would enable these students to be positively included in their school and neighborhood communities. The very first day of training I had decided not to be afraid any longer and to admit when I did not know something even when I was under duress. I was determined to learn everything I could to help my sons and other parents who were willing to learn. When a gentleman, teaching grassroots organizing, asked for a volunteer that first morning, I only remember standing in front of the class. I do not remember walking or, as my classmates told me, running to get up there. I have been running to the front ever since that day learning to do the right thing even when I'm afraid.

During these leadership class sessions, one of the speakers, an older self-advocate named Marv, gave me information that has continued to help us as a family. I spoke to him about my sons and asked for his opinion on the different things I had put in place for them. Marv explained my sons needed a good male psychiatrist. When I questioned the reason for this kind of support, Marv said my sons needed to have a man to talk to about guy stuff. I was a girl and their mom. This meant there would be things they could not talk to me about and I needed to find someone who was a very good person to fill that need for them. He also told me I needed to talk to them about death. Marv, in a quiet voice, shared how no one had taught him about death. He thought his parents would live forever. What wonderful advice! I followed it immediately!

Health Insurance Changes

I had another change in medical insurance which meant I could no longer take Moogie to see the woman doctor at the University's Pediatric Neuropsychiatry Department. The first time we needed to change insurance and find new doctors, we went to a particular hospital and saw a woman psychiatrist who must have failed her college course on patient sympathy and bedside manners. This doctor sat and talked to me about the outcomes she expected for Moogie with Moogie in the room. She told me Moogie would be "severely retarded", needing to be put away. Moogie, playing with the knick knacks on her table, said, "Mom, what is 'tarded?" I told him "retarded" was a class in college in which this doctor received an "A". Taking him by the hand, we left her office.

This same psychiatrist made a medication change for Moogie, stating the new medication would be a better fit for him even though the slow release medication he was currently taking was working fine. When I gave this new medication to Moogie, he became agitated, yelling instead of talking to me. I asked him why he was being rude. He told me the medicine made him mad. I instantly flushed it down the toilet, called the new doctor's office and told the nurse I wanted to come pick up a prescription for Moogie's previous medication. The nurse said that option was not possible. She told me he had to take the new medication and I had to make another appointment with the doctor to discuss a medication change. I took Moogie, on no medication, over to that doctor's office and only gave him one instruction, "Do not leave the clinic"! Then I sat down and read a magazine. Moogie ran through the clinic opening every closed door, twice. Finally, after twenty minutes, the doctor's nurse came to the waiting room and gave me a prescription to renew Moogie's slow release medication. We filled the prescription and went home.

Now this second medical insurance change was happening. It was unnerving. I contacted the doctors at the university where Moogie had received great comprehensive care. I explained to them about the last insensitive doctor we had encountered. Moogie's previous doctor was leaving the university so she contacted a male psychiatrist whom she held in high regards. She told me this doctor was not taking any new patients but she had convinced him to see Moogie by explaining our bad experience with the last insurance change. This psychiatrist accepted all types of insurance. The doctor told me she did not want Moogie to end up with someone who would drug him up causing him to loose his wonderful personality and smile in a fog of medication. We went to this new doctor.

Doctor Bright

We had an 8:00 AM appointment. Arriving on time, we were greeted in the lobby by Dr. Bright who then led us into his office. Dr. Bright was tall and slender and had a very calming voice. Inside his office, he had 3D puzzles and action figures on a low oval coffee table. Moogie was sitting on the floor at the table putting the three dimensional brain puzzle together and taking it apart. When this doctor wanted to talk about things that might hurt Moogie's emotions, he asked Moogie to get water for us from the water cooler in the hallway. I thought this was very thoughtful. After fifteen minutes discussing things with me, the doctor told me he needed to talk to Moogie now. Sitting on the floor opposite Moogie, Dr. Bright asked him one question: "How have you been feeling since you came into my office?" Moogie said, while still playing,"Oooohh, happy, sad, glad and mad". Getting up and sitting back down in his chair, Dr. Bright said we needed to help Moogie get his emotions off the roller coaster ride they were on. He gave him a very mild anti-anxiety medication that was not addictive. The medication worked very well. This doctor was inclusive. He not only listened to me, he also listened to my son. This doctor did not make any medical decisions for my son without informing us of the available choices and discussing how any of the choices we made would be on a trial basis and how it would work on Moogie's body. He taught us what to look for, the good and the bad in the medicines we tried.

New employment

Little did I know my job as a woman's domestic violence advocate was sadly ending. During our weekly staff meetings where advocates shared personal family triumphs and troubles, the executive director appeared to dislike my stories about my children and their ability to overcome their disabilities. I did not understand her attitude towards me. Finally one day, one of the older advocates informed me the executive director had placed her child, with mild disabilities, in a group home - a home where developmentally disabled persons live together when they cannot live at home. My stories were unpleasantly reminding her at our staff meeting every week of that choice she had made. The executive director did not enjoy hearing how well Moogie was doing in his new school placement and what I had learned about our rights in the public school system. I had implemented what I was learning at this setting in order to help children in our shelter; I taught mothers what I learned. The other advocates loved the new information they could use to help their families. However, the executive director disliked my reports so much so she changed the organization's work schedule knowing, as a "single mother", I could not work a 24 hour shift. The change meant I had to look for new employment before I lost this job.

Changing Jobs. . . Again!

After months of unknowingly torturing her every week, the executive director informed me that if I could not work overnights, she could offer me a job in childcare and cut my pay in half. I said thanks, but no thanks. I found a new job in our school district. I was now a "Child Development Technician" or "Teacher's Assistant" in a first year high school Emotional Behavioral Disorder (EBD) class - a class the school principal had tried to stop from entering the building by not hiring staff for it but he had no choice in the matter and the interviews began. My first interview for the position was with the newly hired teacher, Nan, and the school's assistant principal. It lasted ten minutes, ending with my new employment.

Of the twelve students in the EBD class, all were African-American adolescents, one young woman and eleven young men. They entered the classroom on the first day of school and greeted Nan and I coolly as if we were warm lunchmeat. These students watched us with the same distrust I had seen in the eyes of the children at the battered women's shelter; the same look I saw in Moogie's eyes when I told him he had to go to school; the same unsure look in Ray's eyes when I tried to tell him he was bigger than the fly.

These were big people! The height of the males ranged from 5'10" to 6'7" but inside they were still small, frightened children. I was a stranger asking them to share their personal hopes and dreams. Their mistrust was high. When I asked each of them what their dreams were, they gave superficial answers like a pair of name brand tennis shoes or cell phones. Their answers gradually changed, however, as I earned their trust. Before the first winter break, their answers had changed to amazing, well thought out ideas filled with hope of the future, not only to help themselves and their families but their

39

communities, too. Their attitudes were the basis of the African-American culture which is to help not just one, but all. When each of these students began experiencing a crisis in their families, they asked for help and direction.

Building a Trust Bridge

During that first day during lunchtime, I spoke with the teacher, Nan, and told her I would feel better talking to the students' parents. I wanted to hear about the hopes and dreams they had for their young sons and daughter and I wanted parental input on how they wanted me to handle situations when certain behaviors occurred with their children. Nan told me I had her blessings if I wanted to talk to the parents and then wished me good luck in getting very many of them to come to the school to see me. I contacted the parents that day but I did not ask them to come to the school. I asked for their permission to meet them in the community or come to their homes and they all said, yes. I found out home visiting was a good thing and shared that information with the school staff. They decided to follow my lead the following year.

That same first day on my new job, I picked up my children and went to each of the twelve students' homes asking each parent or guardian what they expected from the school for their children. They all gave very clear expectations. I explained how their children could work their way out of this special education program and back into mainstream classes. They signed a paper stating they understood. I had it in writing how to handle their children if their children became upset. We had a process.

The students in this classroom acted with bravado. They were street smart and distrusted authority figures. They always questioned the authenticity of any information presented to them. These students were not used to being involved with their educational process and using positive choices. I found each one of them had untapped strengths: one student could use sign language fluently since his uncle was deaf; another student knew how to write computer code. There was a wide range of abilities and disabilities with only two students fitting the federal and state criteria for an EBD diagnosis. The rest were, according to the law, over-identified.

After the first two months of teaching the boundaries and rules of the classroom and the school, Nan and I found out there was no process in place for these students to work their way out of the EBD program. This exiting process became part of my Partners in Policymaking® class project.   An exiting process was put in place.

Nan and I realized the students first had to understand their own strengths and unique needs. We went through a period being constantly told by administration to get our students into the classroom before the last warning bell. Several of these students became disrespectful to any educator who would tell them to get to class in front of regular education students – behavior always ending in suspension. I asked the class why they all sauntered in or were escorted by a hall monitor into our classroom after the final bell rang? They explained they were ashamed to walk down the hallway leading to our classroom since a black placard with big white letters displaying words screaming, "SPECIAL EDUCATION" was posted over the hallway doors. We worked to get the sign removed. Once it was gone, no one was late to class.

Players

The street definition of Player is ;"They outsmart the smart, cunning, and has street smarts. They know how to get money and [are] skilled at …[getting] it" (Urban dictionary). I challenged the entire class to watch "*Shindler's List*", a very long two-part movie about the Jewish Holocaust. The hook I used for the students was this: I declared that if they were such "players", why were they were living with their moms and none of them working a job? I told them I knew of a real player who started with one suit, a ring and a gold watch, turning nothing into millions of dollars. The teacher told me if I could get these students to watch a black and white movie that did not have hip-hop music in it, she would let me try my next idea with no questions asked.

The next day, I brought the movie to school and put it in the VCR. It was somewhat funny to see every single student finally come into class alert and equipped with paper and pencil ready to take notes so they could become a "real player". This showed me they knew how to be prepared for learning which is exactly what they needed to do in order for them to be successful citizens.

I watched an amazing metamorphose occur. As the movie played, I saw these hard core "emotional behavior and disabled" students change. They changed the same way the person, Shindler, changed by looking at right and wrong and becoming compassionate and caring. They cried when the little girl in the red coat who had hidden from the Nazis, was burned on a pile of other tortured Jewish bodies. We finished watching the second half of the movie the following day. Nan and I received complements from the librarian and several English teachers who stated our students had presented incredible insights about the Holocaust to them.

My next task was to teach them a lesson in American History, a very dry history about the Quakers and the English. With the blessings of Nan, I decided to liven up the lesson. We, as a class, undertook the lesson subject: "Deborah Sampson", a woman serving in the Continental Army in the Revolutionary war. Deborah Sampson disguised herself as a man. We decided to do a skit of the story in the format of a "Jerry Springer" show (1998). It was a hilarious skit. The student who knew sign language signed the script and we taped it in the high school's television studio. They were not bad actors, not bad at all.

Changing Behavior Without Belittling The Student

Manny, the young man who played Jerry Springer in our class skit, had a heart-breaking smile but, he cursed every other word. It was like breathing for him. I went back to his home and spoke to his mother, grandmother and great-grandmother. They were very receptive to me but did not know how to stop his use of abusive language in public since he did not use bad language in their presence. As we sat, trying to brainstorm on his abuse of the English language, three of his uncles came in swearing like drunken sailors. No, they were not really drunk but I realized now how Manny thought using cuss words was a strong and "manly" thing to do. This gave me a baseline from which to start. Here was a young man who wanted a summer job and prided himself in how he dressed. Therefore, I took Manny to a prestigious clothing store and spoke with the human resource (HR) person, with whom I had already had a conversation beforehand. Manny was excited about the possibility of working at this department store for the summer. In front of Manny, I asked the HR person if it was acceptable for their employees to use curse words while working. Of course the HR person went into a big spew about how that kind of behavior would not be acceptable because it would drive customers away, causing the loss of money for the store. It worked! Manny learned his lesson quickly without telling him he was bad, without telling him he was not able to do the job, or without warning him he had better stop using bad language. Manny worked at the store that summer, never cursing ... not in front of customers anyway.

The only young woman in the class had a "B" grade point average and faired well in a male dominated classroom. We had hoped to have another young woman in the classroom so she would not feel alone. Clyde, the EBD program's social worker, did not want to put the new student in our classroom because she was Caucasian. Instead, he put her in a class for the developmentally disabled. She began skipping school. By chance, I saw this young woman entering a house that sold drugs and housed prostitutes. I immediately gave this information to Clyde who told me the student had run away from home. She was found, months later, in the state of Tennessee dancing in a strip club, strung out on drugs. I cannot help but wonder if she had had the emotional behavioral support and resources would she still have run away.

Visual learners

The school year finally ended and summer was upon us. The discovery of a wonderful teaching tool named visual/spatial intelligence was uncovered, totally by accident. During the first week of summer vacation, I became enlightened about both of my sons' learning window. I bought Walt Disney's version of *Mary Poppins* for my children and they all loved it. From that, I discovered Ray and Moogie watched life as if it were a movie. In fact, one afternoon they showed me exactly how they learned. Both of them are persons with developmental disabilities and were thrilled to watch the movie three times in a row.

We decided to take a ride to the Dairy Queen with visions of butterscotch-dipped ice cream cones on our minds. As we drove to get our treat, my sons started speaking the dialog in the *Mary Poppins'* movie with precision and clarity. They did not miss a word in the script; they sang using the exact intonation and accents they had heard in the songs. While reenacting the movie they would even laugh at the parts they thought were funny. This ability of my sons to remember pretty much everything they heard and saw, spurred me on to become the gatherer of family movies. Finding African-American family movies was difficult, but I found many other great movies. I bought as many movies as I could that mirrored little boys my sons' ages; I bought other movies that taught empathy, social skills, love, heartbreak, and the good, the bad and the ugly - absolutely no horror was allowed! We found family stories, mysteries, and bible cartoons. Of course Batman and Robin, and Superman movies were necessary, too. This was also the time I discovered I needed to remove the television antennae. One evening after dinner dishes were finished, we sat down to watch a sit com. When the show began, one of the characters called another character a female dog

("B_tch"). Unbelievable! I did not need my children to imitate and repeat language like this in school that they were never allowed to utter in our home.

I found ways for us to keep busy at home. For Ray and Moogie's fine motor deficits, I had them cut coupons, help make biscuits, work with play dough and color pictures to make their learning fun. I also bought one of the earliest video game systems and tried to get the games to match the movies we bought. In that way, we could play the games, share our thoughts and feelings with one another, and talk about what was happening. We discussed what the characters were doing and why some things they did were good and others things they did were not so good. My children were strong visual learners; the window through which I could teach them the world. That summer the daycare told me everyday how wonderful and quickly my children's social skills were progressing. How affirming for me to know that the visual learning was working for them!

Teaching Turmoil

When the next school year came, I found the Emotional Behavioral Disorder (EBD) teacher had changed. It turned out last year's teacher, Nan, had been having mini seizures all year long and only came back to teach because of her earnings. Her salary as a special education teacher was more than an assistant principal was being paid. She showed me her contract. Betsy, the newly hired EBD teacher, was a teacher who acquired her license in that area because she already had a degree and could grandfather into the licensure. There was one problem with Betsy as an EBD educator. She was afraid of all the students except for one fourteen year old, ninth grade student named Rome. Rome, who stood six feet four inches tall, was a football player and loved reading Dr. Seuss books during class free time. I, on the other hand, believed Rome to be the most dangerous student/person I had ever encountered in my life. Rome showed no emotion; not happiness when he was happy and no visible signs of anger when he was very upset. Reading his student file, I did not understand his placement in this setting without the necessary supports that had been identified in his comprehensive evaluation.

This was the year the building principal moved the EBD classroom downstairs in the basement, across from the lunchroom and away from the rest of the student body. This new location did not help their self-esteem since the students were now feeling thrown away and no longer a part of the school. The principle's rationale was that these EBD students were always late to class anyway so it didn't matter. Perhaps he did not understand how the sign that read "Special Education", which was posted over the hallway leading to the classroom where we had previously been, was shaming to teenagers. After all, it was better to be a "bad boy", than a boy who needed special education services. Mix this combination of negative ingredients together: one scared teacher with detached, disappointed, and hopeless students who have been misevaluated and misplaced in an EBD special education classroom, and the result is an inevitable pot about to explode.

A dangerous incident occurred the very first time ever in the EBD classroom. It happened the day Betsy, our new EBD teacher, promised Rome he could eat his lunch in the classroom after he had confided in her that three football players threatened to beat him up if he showed up to eat lunch in the cafeteria. Betsy offered this safe haven to Rome even though there was a rule in the school forbidding eating in the classroom because of rodents. Lunchtime arrived. Rome went through the lunch line and returned to the classroom to eat where he had been invited for safety reasons. There he found Betsy standing in the classroom doorway talking to the head principal, who was an unexpected guest at the time. Rome was turned away. He returned to the cafeteria to eat his lunch where the football players beat him in the head. After the attack, the huge battered Rome returned to the classroom where he began calmly telling Betsy she knew he would get beat up at lunch. As he talked, his anger and frustration escalated. He began throwing furniture across the room horizontally with such force the pieces hit the wall and crumbled. At this point, I walked into the classroom. Rome never raised his voice and his facial expression never changed as he slowly inched his way towards Betsy telling her his headache pain was all her fault. Picking up a rack of books, he sailed them across the room hitting the wall and bouncing off like ping pong balls. I immediately walked between them and began yelling at him to tell me what happened. His eyes turned to me and he began telling me what had occurred as he slowly walked towards me. Immediately I started walking backwards, keeping eye contact with him while moving into the hallway. Rome followed me telling me how he did what Betsy had instructed him to do but she left him hanging. He softly explained Betsy told a lie in front of the head principal; she swore she never told him he could eat in the classroom. This student did not understand Betsy was just trying to get the principal to move away from her room so he could come back and eat in there. I understood the urgency of moving this young man out of the school hallway before the first bell rang and the halls would be filled with unsuspecting students. I felt like a pied piper blowing a horn tied to explosives that could blow any second. As Rome followed my voice, he began punching the concrete walls in the hallway. I could hear the crunching sound of his fist over his calm voice. Every door we passed Rome would level powerful punches. He punched out the cafeteria wire windows in the metal doors but still followed me out of the building telling and retelling his story like a demented battery operated toy that did not have an off button. Only one assistant principal came to assist me. He walked with a cane. After I waved him away, no other adult came to help. After thirty minutes, we stopped walking around the school parking lot; Rome stopped talking. Looking at me with a facial expression that never changed, he stated he did not know we had ever left the classroom or the school building. Calmly, I asked Rome if he would come back into school with me so he could make a report to the school police liaison officer about the lunch room attack on him. He politely agreed. I reported the incident and my conclusions about the student's placement to the assistant principal who had tried to assist me during the crisis.

After that incident, I found myself in another predicament. Betsy had no cultural or behavioral training and now it appeared she was afraid of losing her job since she had not handled this student correctly. Consequently, Betsy, along with the EBD social worker, Clyde, who had not done his job evaluating the records of this student for placement, filed a complaint against me stating I had divided the classroom by polarizing it into a black and white racial situation.

A couple of years later, Betsy apologized to me explaining how Clyde had pressured her into writing that letter against me. Afraid of losing her job, she wrote it. At least that was her report as she apologized to me about my removal from the classroom to the in school suspension room. People will do strange things when they make mistakes and are afraid to deal with the consequences. What is surprising is that these same people do not think children learn from modeled behavior - the old "do as I say, not as I do" group.

51

In School Suspension

My employment placement in the school system changed. I was still a Child Development Technician (CDT) but was moved from the EBD classroom to the in school suspension (ISS) room. I missed the EBD students. They missed me also. So much so they started acting out just to be sent to the in school suspension room where I was working. They told me the new CDT in their EBD classroom, a young African-American woman, was gang affiliated and only one of their classmates had had gang affiliation before she came. It was not safe for them in the classroom any more. I learned from these students how the EBD classroom had been a safe haven for all of the different gang members in the room. We had a truce there which was known only by all the members of that classroom. What was talked about in the classroom stayed in the classroom. Not anymore. The balance was removed by an open show of gang affiliation by the new CDT. Regardless of who their new support person was and whether or not she truly *was* a gang member or simply using that information thinking it would help her develop a better trust with the students, I had to stop these horrible choices the students were making. Missing their classes and getting into trouble in order to be sent to the in school suspension room to see me, was not a good choice. How are students supposed to handle such stress? School is supposed to provide a learning environment, a safe place to make childish mistakes. Students should neither have to come into a school to fight people who are supposed to be public servants nor should they have to worry about jail or probation officers because of school truancy. I told the EBD students how smart and strong I thought they were, explaining that, if they could maneuver through the dangerous situations out on the street and arrive home safely each day, the game of gaining an education should be like cutting a piece of cake for them. I challenged them one more time to use their strengths and work their way out of the EBD Program and many of them did. With permission from an assistant principal, these same students began visiting me between their classes, and before and after school.

That spring, when our high school principal moved me to the in school suspension room, the Columbine High (cb) School shootings took place. We were instructed to talk about this tragic event with the students in our classes during second hour. At the time of the announcement, I had nine students in the suspension room with me. We read the newspaper article about the shootings together; we had an interactive conversation. The students explained to me that the entire event was the Columbine school administration's fault. When I questioned how they had come to that conclusion, this was their explanation: the week before the shootings, one of the student shooters had held a loaded gun to a student's head. The only punishment meted out for that action was one day school suspension and his parents had to take the gun home with them! One of my students blurted out that when she had merely said, "That's booty!" she received a two day suspension. She asked why these Columbine students continually received such miniscule punishments for dangerous actions, especially with zero tolerance in effect. The students all agreed it was because they were rich, male, and white. I had both white and black students in my class and they all agreed on this point. They continued to explain how the Columbine shooters had exhibited escalating behavior all year long.

These shooters had not felt as though they were part of the high school; they had no self-esteem; they were not jocks and were not part of any "in" crowd. Since these Columbine shooters did not belong anywhere and thought they were invisible, they accepted and embraced their invisibility to the point of planning the death of other students as well as their own. Their invisibility is what the students blamed on administration.

Just as I had finally asked my son, Ray, the right question ("How big is the fly?") in order to see how he interpreted his environment, I questioned these students sitting in the in school suspension room. I asked them if they were concerned about a similar incident happening in their high school environment. In an uproar, I heard a chorus of voices answer, "No, not at all!" Very interested in their reasoning, I asked, "Why not here?" The students assuredly told me a Columbine incident could never occur here because the first time any student put a loaded gun to another student's head and did not shoot, it would leave them no other choice but to take matters into their own hands. They would not depend on school administration to know what was happening in the school's environment. Why? Because the students claimed our administration was too busy playing politics for money and positioning themselves in the district for promotions and retirement. These students went on to explain how many gang fights and threats happen everyday where school staff turn their heads claiming not to see what had taken place or were naïve and did not understand the gestures and interactions they had just witnessed. To protect themselves, these students would beat and break the trigger fingers of anyone who attended their school and had the mental instability to hold a gun to someone's head. This beating would occur every time the gun-toting student was allowed to return to school. Not quite the answer I had anticipated, but it was to the point.

I had a visit in the in school suspension room from a student who I had never seen in trouble before. That day he stated he was suspended from school but had decided to come anyway. It seemed he had called the fire department informing them that he knew none of the automatic fire alarms were working in the school because they had all been turned off. The principal had deemed the alarms were too expensive to have on even though we had a firebug in the school that year.

As we talked, this student also informed me he was part of a "set", a newly formed gang. I asked him why he would want to be part of a group of people that had the intent of wrongdoing on their minds. I tried to impress upon him that the African-American community needed more positive leaders who would lead us in the right direction. This young man informed me he hung out at the house with the son of the current school administrator where many other district leaders also hung out. This young man told me he was learning from one of the best gangs when he hung out there. That sent chills up my spine.

Another day a very disgruntled and angry group of students came into the in school suspension room. These were students I had never seen before. When we finally processed through their problems, I sent for the principal. It seems there had been a job fair at school that day. When it was over, these students had gone back to their Spanish class and were given a joke to translate by their teacher. The joke ended with the line "Welcome to Nigga's row". An eruption occurred in the classroom with the students yelling at the teacher stating she was wrong to say racist things of any kind. For their actions, the students were all suspended for the rest of that class period. Had these students been supported for what had occurred in their classroom or at least been given a process to follow if this reoccurred? No! They were not given a safety process but at least the teacher was moved to another school at the natural break of the quarter.

During this time, I was in the process of going through the Governor Council's leadership training program. I was learning about rights that could be used in many systems, including education. I innocently believed professionals at my school did not understand they could *not* punish students with disabilities if the behavior pertained to their disability unless they followed the processes written in the special education law (Individuals with Disabilities Education Act or IDEA). I asked the school social worker if he knew we could get in huge trouble if the State Education Agency was aware we had incomplete student files, students who were suspended because of their disabilities with no Individual Education Plan in place, and students who were over-identified for special education services? I asked the right question ("How big is the fly?") to make them aware of their environment but little did I realize I also opened a Pandora's Box. Clyde, along with other special education staff, knew the law. They knew these processes were illegal and now I was a threat to them. These professionals taught me a lesson. They conveniently lost my summer school job placement papers and thereby ended my employment with the public school system. I now had to scuffle to find work so I could feed my children and keep our home.

New Job, Bad Daycare

During a stressful summer, I lost our car because I was two payments behind. It was also the time of my daughter's thirteenth birthday and I had to leave her alone at home all summer. I felt horrible!

Our wonderful daycare center told me my daughter was aging out so I found another daycare who would take all of my children. The woman who ran that daycare in her home used to be a coworker of mine. I believed she would treat my children with compassion and love. She turned out to be a monster.

I learned about the horror stories and events my children and others had to survive in this dungeons and dragons day care. This woman pushed Moogie and a two year old down her basement steps; then claimed it was due to their clumsiness. She pinched them during naptime to threaten them into silence and then covered their heads with a blanket. Moogie and Gavin stopped liking bedtime "tuck-in" due to her unloving abuse. Moogie felt unsafe at his daycare. I learned this woman underfed my sons, which explained their new behavior of gorging and hoarding food at home. She made them stand outside in the hot July sun; no sitting in the shade allowed! When it was too hot, she would make them stand on the park's baseball mound while she sat in her new truck with the air conditioner running. This explained why on hot days my sons were dehydrated. Whenever I brought food for my children, the daycare provider ate it. When I gave her money for fast food, she would order a complete fast food meal for herself and one order of fries to split between my three sons. This was to be their lunch for the day.

I found out what was happening when Moogie began running away from the daycare just like he ran away from school, only this time I received a call from our neighborhood hardware store where I took my children when we bought house-fixing supplies. The man told me Moogie was there with him. When my ex-coworker, now daycare provider, showed up to get him, the man would not let Moogie go with her. He said he got a bad feeling from "that woman". That night I rolled out printing paper and drew pictures with my children. I had to stifle the screams that welled up inside of me as they drew the abuse they and the other children had to endure every day while we parents thought they were in safe keeping. I removed my children immediately from her so-called "care" and wrote a complaint to the county daycare licensing office.

Under the gun from the retaliation I had just experienced through the school district, I gained new employment with an educational advocacy center. It was the receptionist there who sent me my first packet of information on our rights under state laws that were aligned with the federal government's "Individuals with Disabilities Education Act" and "The Americans with Disabilities Act".

When I had attended my second interview for this job, the executive director offered me an advocate's job and I accepted it. An African-American co-worker came into the main building after I began employment there. She told me she had to see if it was true that a "dark skinned sister" was actually working in the "big house". Okay, I wondered, what had I gotten myself into this time? Even though her comments made me skeptical, I still could not believe I was advocating for families for pay!

Asked to attend an evening board meeting soon after starting my new advocate job, I had to pick up my three sons, get them home, change my clothes, and return to work. I am a person who began to believe that everything happens for a reason and this was one of those times. I drove home to ask my daughter DeeDee if she wanted to ride with me to pick up her brothers but she was not there. Yes, I was perturbed. Having this mandatory meeting I needed to know she would be there to care for her brothers.

As I drove to the daycare alone, a big green car came out of nowhere driving thirty miles an hour parallel to my car. The driver suddenly turned left into me and hit me, broad-siding my car on the passenger's side. Smashing in the entire door, seat, frame, and tire well, both of my airbags were instantly set off. That was the day I learned those soft-looking, puffy airbags shown in car commercials were not the ones installed in my car! I had the course burlap bags shooting out at me at 200 miles an hour, propelled by a single shotgun shell. I should have asked the right question when I bought the car (How big is the fly?) so I knew about my environment and how the airbags in my car worked! No wonder it is dangerous for short persons and small infants to sit in the front seat of autos with airbags. No one would/could tell me why it took the automobile companies so long to decide the safety issue of these airbags for small individuals and inform the public of their danger; because …? My airbags not only deployed but caught on fire. The police and ambulance arrived to find me with bruises and burns. I was seeing everything as if I was looking through a tunnel … as if I was looking through a circular lens of a one-eyed binocular. At the time, I experienced no pain. I refused an ambulance ride to the hospital, but, being a *single parent,* I still needed to find a way to transport my children home. I did not want them sent to emergency foster care because I had abandoned them at a daycare center. Looking at my crumpled car, I was, at that moment, glad DeeDee had lingered after school or at a girlfriend's house before coming home. If she had been at home and agreed to ride along with me, she would have been burned and intertwined with the twisted metal of what was left of our car. Everything does happen for a reason!

Shortly after I refused the ambulance ride, I phoned my job supervisor from a local community center situated at the corner where the accident had happened. I explained to her what had transpired. She said she would go to the evening meeting in my place. Then I phoned a friend of our family who came to pick me up at the scene of the accident and drove onward to pick up my sons who were at daycare. This friend brought us all home. When DeeDee arrived home that day, she found me standing in the front door of our house waiting for her to come home safely. She told me where she had been. She asked me where our car was and I informed her about the accident and about my tunnel vision. She told me I *had* to go to the hospital and then called my neighborhood sister who drove me there. This devastating car accident included many doctor appointments. I could not lie down to sleep. Moogie would bring his blanket and pillow downstairs and sleep at my feet. He was afraid my time was up ... that I would die. At school, Moogie told his teachers and friends about my car accident and they gave him wonderful support.

Flight

One afternoon at school, Moogie tried to tell school staff that there was a boy hurting a little girl on the playground. The staff did not listen to him so he went over and pulled the boy off the crying girl. The staff saw him do this and went over to Moogie, grabbed him by the arm and pulled him into the school. Even with the little girl's help, it took a long time for the staff to figure out that Moogie had actually come to her rescue and saved her. I do not know how long it took the staff to unravel what had happened! That day I had a neurologist's appointment on the south side of town. During my office visit was when I received a call on my cell phone from my daughter who told me she had Moogie on the house phone and he was lost. He had left the school and was trying to come home but became lost and stuck.

Moogie was sitting on the sidewalk squarely in front of an elderly couple's home. They knew something was wrong. When the elderly man came out and asked Moogie if he needed help, Moogie put his hand up, in stop sign fashion, stating he was lost and did not talk to strangers. The man and his wife took their cordless phone out to Moogie and placed it on the sidewalk square, right next to the square where Moogie sat rooted. He called home. I drove from the south side to the city's north side, ending up at the cross street Moogie had spelled out to his sister. I was so relieved to see him sitting down in his square eating cookies and milk from the kind, elderly woman. She had given them to him to keep him from walking away until I arrived. After thanking them and promising a dinner certificate to their favorite restaurant, I drove Moogie back to school. School personnel had not noticed Moogie was gone and had wandered over 10 blocks away. When we arrived, they had just understood how Moogie had not been fighting on the playground but had been helping this little girl fend off her attacker.

One paraprofessional approached Moogie telling him he needed to be more responsible and stop running away. I stopped her and asked her why she deemed what had occurred on the playground with Moogie was any of her business? She turned and walked away. It turned out, according to Moogie, this was the same para who was supposed to be watching the children outside but was engaged in a conversation with several other adults and not tending to any of the children. The school decided to put a single one-on-one paraprofessional with Moogie instead of having a shared aid.

A Good Book

Ray was now in middle school. At his Individual Education Plan (IEP) meeting, it was discussed how he would leave his regular education class for small group reading. I objected to having him pulled out for reading since he was already leaving his class for speech. I thought once was enough. I told the team I would supplement his reading at home. My reasoning was clear: Ray learned on the autism spectrum and had a unique auditory processing need. When giving information to Ray, teachers needed to use very few words. This information was included in his IEP because of the auditory processing lag time. Sound goes into his ears and then takes several seconds to process before the sound is heard. Nevertheless, whenever he learned a routine, he no longer needed assistance. I wanted him to change classes with his class and learn this routine while allowing the other students to get used to seeing him with his class. Ray was very big, but gentle. The school district provided a one-on-one para for him because of Ray's naiveté.

One day, someone decided Ray's para would take her break during silent reading time in his English class. It might have worked out well for Ray but no one explained this change in the process to him. The English teacher felt confident she could direct Ray without the para's assistance. She might have been able to help Ray understand what she wanted if she had first read one page called "Portrait of Ray" that summarized his strengths and unique needs. I had provided copies of this page to everyone so that busy teachers, especially substitutes, could teach class and not have to read his entire IEP.

As English class began, the teacher told the students to pick a "good" book from the table situated in the front of the room. Return to their desks and read silently. The teachers request to obtain a "good" book caused a problem for Ray. He stood at the table trying to find a book that was "good". How does one know if the book is "good"? Ray, looking at the books lined up on the table, started on the left side and began reading the backs of each book to help him determine which were the "good" ones! After ten minutes and only having read the backs of three books, his teacher impatiently told him to just pick any book and sit down. This caused Ray to loose where he was in analyzing which book could possibly be "good" for him to take, so he had to start his processing from the beginning again. His classmates laughed. They knew what Ray was doing. After all, many of them attended elementary school and were now in middle school with him. Several of the students asked to assist the teacher in explaining the situation to Ray. Being the teaching professional she was, however, she turned down their offers. His classmates were Ray's natural supports. They knew every time the teacher would interrupt Ray, he would start his processing over from the beginning. Ray was embarrassed but he continued his process of looking on the back of each book starting from the left side of the table. Finally, the teacher told him to sit down immediately! Not yet, he thought to himself. He did not have his "good" book like everyone else. Ray put his hand up in stop sign fashion at the teacher and asked her to be quiet. In fact he said, "Close your mouth, you have too many words." The more she talked, the more confusing it was for Ray. The teacher thought Ray was being disrespectful and called for a hall monitor, who in turn called the social worker, who in turn called the autism teacher. They all descended on Ray in his classroom. Surrounding Ray in the front of the classroom were three adults, all talking at the same time, which made it impossible for Ray to hear anything they were saying clearly. And, more importantly, he did not understand why they were there in the first place! I wish someone would have thought to ask Ray the right question (How big is the fly?) so they could understand what was happening to him in his environment!

A concerned classmate who had been in school with Ray since third grade took a chance and slipped out of the classroom amidst the chaos. He ran to find Ray's para, explaining to her what was happening in English class. The para immediately came and ordered the other adults to back away. She asked Ray to follow her and they left the room. Ray walked slowly with his head held low, tears dropping silently from his big brown eyes, showing all the signs of disappointment, of failure. She took him to the cafeteria where he slumped in one of the plastic sway back chairs weeping. Ray explained he was trying to find the "good" book as his teacher had instructed. He told his aid how the teacher started using too many words, too fast. He asked her if he could call me; he asked *me* if he could come home because his head was hurting. I picked him up and took him home.

After that incident, we had a meeting at the school where it was decided Ray's para would take her breaks after the first fifteen or twenty minutes of class to make sure the instructions were clear to him before she left the room. After implementing this process, Ray did not have any more unwelcome behaviors in his classes. In fact, that year, Ray took a Japanese language class in which he did not need any help and he received the highest grade in the class. We discovered he understood Japanese better than he understood English since Japanese is a concrete language with no need to use too many words!

Schoolwork or Homework

Moogie, now in fifth grade, decided he did not need to do any more class work or homework. It appears his teacher explained how people go to school and do class work and homework until they understand the lesson being taught. Since Moogie believed he knew the material once he left his class, he thought he no longer needed to do any more work either in class *or* at home. For that reason, he would play a video game about a hedgehog for thirty minutes, like clockwork, when he came home from school. I noticed Moogie was definitely refusing to do any homework that was truly unfinished class work that he had brought home with him. I knew this could become either a nightly battle or I could come up with an idea to give the school power over his video game. Buying a tiny padlock at the dollar store, I put this lock through one of the holes in the prongs of the power cord for the game. The game system was locked. Moogie asked me what had happened? Where was the key? I explained to him that the only way I could unlock his game was if he finished all of his work. He would have to earn "hedgehog tickets" at school for the work he finished in each of his classes. The tickets paid Moogie in ten minute game time increments; he bought into it. He would bring home his tickets and earn up to fifty minutes of uninterrupted, blissful video game time. Moogie liked the ticket system in which he did not have to share the game with anyone during his ticket time. After three weeks, he did not need the ticket incentives any more to do his schoolwork. It had become a habit.

Moogie had learned to follow school rules in middle school by the sixth grade. In fact, he loved to go to middle school. I found out much later he had had a girl friend. They had decided they were boyfriend and girlfriend even though they never phoned each other. In fact, they only waved at each other in the hallways between classes.

Moogie broke up with her when he saw her plant a kiss on another boy's cheek. He informed me his heart must be broken because it hurt. He asked if there was any medicine to help. We talked about feelings and how they can hurt just like a physical injury.

School Safety with Injuries

In seventh grade, I received a phone call from the middle school health nurse, Sandy, who informed me there had been an accident outside and she believed Moogie was having an asthma attack. When I asked her what he was doing, she stated he was staring off into space, no spitting and no wheezing. I knew by this description he was not having an asthma attack. Something else was wrong. They sent him to Children's Hospital by ambulance and I met him there. Moogie saw me but did not acknowledge me. The autism specialist was with him. She, too, tried to tell me he was having an asthma attack but I could see he was not having trouble breathing. The doctor came into the examination room and began questioning Moogie who was unresponsive. After almost two hours, Moogie sat up and asked how he had gotten to the hospital. The doctor questioned Moogie asking him what was the last thing he remembered. Moogie told everyone in the room how his class had been outside playing basketball. He turned to make a jump shot when another student knocked his feet out from under him. Moogie fell down flat on his back, hitting his head. He told the doctor he went to sleep and woke up just now in the emergency room. The doctor announced that Moogie had suffered a traumatic brain injury. The TBI diagnosis confirmed my belief of him not having an asthma attack. Then I questioned where his para was during his fall at school? No one knew. Because of that incident, we met as an individual education planning team and wrote Moogie's three step School Safety Plan:

> *<u>Step one</u>: Moogie was to ask his paraprofessional to take him to see his safe person when experiencing high anxiety that would make him want to run home.*

> *<u>Step two</u>: Moogie was to ask for the social worker who was his first safe person contact. With orders from the principal, he would be allowed to wait for the social worker.*

> *<u>Step three</u>: Moogie was to go to the autism resource room where he could call me.*

The next time I received a call about Moogie being injured in middle school was during his eighth grade year. The nurse called telling me there had been an accident and Moogie's leg was bleeding. She had slowed the bleeding down but it would not quit. I asked her why they had not sent him to the hospital if he was still bleeding. Her response was because then the school would have to pay for the ambulance.

Angry and fearing how much blood was flowing, I picked Moogie up and took him to the hospital emergency room. He told me, as we drove, he was never going back to school ever again. While the doctors put twenty-seven stitches in his leg, Moogie told us the story of what had occurred. It seemed all of the eighth grade teachers had taken the entire eighth grade class to the gymnasium. The students played floor hockey at the same time the teachers played basketball and while the two paraprofessionals were in a corner of the gym engaged in a conversation. In other words, none of the public servants, teachers or aids, were watching the students.

Moogie was very good at floor hockey. His team was winning. Moogie hit the puck. Instead of it going into the net, it ricocheted off the metal goal post, hitting another eighth grader in the chest. Moogie apologized to him but this student did not accept the apology. Picking up the puck enraged, the student began beating Moogie in the head with it. Several students in Moogie's class, including his friend Allan, pulled the student off. The teachers did not respond to the ruckus; they continued to play hoops. In pain and filled with anxiety, Moogie went into the locker room where he cried and used curse words. He said the attacking student followed him into the room. Moogie picked up a metal pole. Growling and cussing, he swung the pole repeatedly at the student. The student ran out of the room. Moogie, wanting to come home, began to follow the safety plan the school and I had put together with him and for him. These were the same steps the school professionals had promised him they would follow. When he did not feel safe, Moogie had promised not to run away from the school but would follow the steps of this plan and this is just what he tried to do.

> *Step one: Moogie asked his paraprofessional to take him to see his safe person. When he asked her, his paraprofessional told him to wait, class was almost over. With anxiety at a very high level, he left the gym alone without his one-on-one paraprofessional noticing. He left and went to the main office.*

> *Step two: Asking for his first safe person contact, Moogie walked into the school's main office and asked for the social worker. (Instructions had been given to the front office by the principal to allow all students, not just Moogie, to wait for the social worker.) Upon his arrival at the front desk, staff told him he had to go back to class because the social worker was not in his office.*

> *Step three: Go to the autism resource room where he could call me. Moogie, trying to keep his promise to me, then went to the autism resource room only to find a locked door.*

By this time Moogie's anxiety level had reached a flight response. He thought about how he had promised me not to put his *hands* on the door of the school leaving to come home to a place where he felt safe. Looking at his current situation, he found a solution: nothing was said about using his *feet* to push the metal bar on the glass door that would open the door to freedom for him. Pushing the bar with his right foot, his shoe slipped on the smooth metal bar and continued through the glass door, slicing his leg open.

The doctors at Children's Hospital emergency room told him how very proud they were of him for not fighting the student. One doctor told Moogie he did not know whether or not he could have withstood an attack of being repeatedly hit in the head with a hockey puck and not automatically fight back. Moogie said going to school was hell! The doctors laughed. I knew Moogie was serious. Moogie feared school but he also knew about the compulsory attendance law which I had to read to him at least once a week. Moogie did not want to break any laws. I contacted a lawyer I thought was a friend. I was told Moogie had a tort claim against the school district. This lawyer, however, never followed through with the tort claim declaring she had lost the copies of Moogie's records.

Middle school was not all bad for Moogie. He made friends in regular education *and* special education classes. One of Moogie's friends, Allan, had invited him to a school overnight camping trip. On this outing, Allan told Moogie all about girls and how to become friends with them. They had lots of fun together. His friend, Allan, taught him a lot about being a middle school student and how to stay away from people who say they are your friend but are not. Allan, a regular education student, stayed at our home on weekends. He convinced Moogie that vegetables were the body's friend. Allan told me he liked Moogie. He said my son was a great friend. One time when he stayed at our home, he told me how he had befriended Moogie during lunchtime. Allan watched Moogie secretly give half of his food to a hungry student who did not have money to buy his own lunch. The next time he watched Moogie, Allan stated how he saw bullies taking this hungry student's lunch away from him right under the noses of school staff. Finally Moogie stood up and told the bullies to get away from the special education student who could not fight for his lunch. The bullies started to surround Moogie and Allan stepped up beside him telling them they would have to fight them both. As most cowards do, when they saw Moogie was not alone, they backed off, leaving the hungry student alone to eat his lunch. The result of this human event was that Moogie and Allan became great friends. Moogie went over to Allan's house where they caught the city bus and went out to the local mall where they got stranded. When they realized they had spent all their monies and could not take the bus back to Allan's house, they called me. I, of course, picked them up. I cried on my way to get them. Moogie, who professionals said could never do regular things, was hanging out at the mall with a friend he had made because of his good character

70

Pioneer

When Ray was a freshman in high school, I met with his case manager who informed me Ray could not take regular classes and receive regular grades because *it had never been done* at that school. This special education case manger's statement reminded me of Rays IEP transition meeting from eighth grade to high school ... one of the few meetings Ray would ever want to attend. At that meeting, a person in the school district tried to convince Ray to attend a high school over south proclaiming that's where higher functioning autistic students attend. This district person asked Ray if he *truly* wanted to attend the high school over northeast, take *regular* classes and work for *regular* grades. Ray thought about her question while I observed the partially hidden smiles of his eighth grade middle school teachers who were warmly awaiting Ray's answer. Ray spoke directly to the district woman stating, since he lived in a regular home, in a regular neighborhood, attended a regular church and shopped at regular grocery stores, yes, he wanted to take regular classes and work for regular grades!

Then Ray added something that made all the adults stop and marvel at the wonderful person he is. He said he had a friend on the autism spectrum in middle school who would only venture out of the autism resource room if Ray would take him for a walk. This student would be going to the same high school Ray had chosen to attend. Ray asked the district person if she believed his friend should also come out of the high school autism resource room to see high school. Ray enrolled in the high school of his choice.

Ray's high school case manager explained to us that pass/fail grades were mandated by the building principal for all special education students. I immediately called a meeting with both the principal

71

and the case manager. In the meeting, I pointed out how my son had always received grades for his schoolwork and changing this process would affect both his motivation and his self-esteem. The principal explained that students in special education must receive pass/fail grades for this reason: if the only regular education class a special education student ever took while they were in high school would be an art class, they could accidentally be awarded cum laude of their class. I asked if it was the computer or school staff who chose the cum laude person of the senior class. The principal stopped and then stated I was correct on both counts. True, the computer kicked out the names but staff overviewed students' academic records and chose the person to be cum laude. Once again I had asked the right question, "How big is the fly?", and Ray could now receive regular grades in his high school classes. The case manager was neither happy with this decision nor with the fact that Ray would have a class schedule consisting of all mainstream classes. Remember, *never had it been done* at this school before; Ray was the first. He did not have to go down into the basement and be in the autism resource classroom.

For the first three weeks, Ray wandered around and attended his classes by himself but they were not productive for him. Then on Friday evening of the third week of school, I received a phone call from one of the assistant principals who dealt with students in special education. Assistant Principal Danube politely informed me Ray would be suspended the following Monday, Tuesday, and Wednesday due to unwelcome behavior on a school field trip. She went on to explain how Ray and four other students had decided to play tag in an art museum, causing one of the expensive paintings to fall off the wall and damaging the frame. Danube commended Ray for being truthful and admitting he was playing tag with the other students. I waited patiently as Danube explained the whys of her decision. Then I asked her where was Ray's one-on-one paraprofessional during this time? Assistant Principal Danube paused and asked if Ray was a student in special education. At that I replied yes, and said he was not to go anywhere without his one-on-one para. Danube asked if she could call me back later that same evening and I agreed. When

I received the second phone call, Ray's suspension no longer existed because there had not been a paraprofessional with him. Danube told me Ray could come back to school on Monday but I did not agree with that decision. We talked further and came to the agreement that, even though his educational support staff was not in place that day, Ray would miss one day of school since he had been involved in running and playing tag inside the art museum. Ray understood he should be suspended since his actions were against school rules. Allowing him to take responsibility for his actions actually made him feel a part of the school. He felt he should receive consequences for doing something he later found out was wrong and be suspended the same as the other students.

A True Friend

One of the students, who did not like the fact that Ray had told Assistant Principal Danube the truth about who was involved in the art museum incident and how it had happened, plotted to get back at Ray. The young man responsible for bumping the painting in an attempt not to be tagged, was an Asian student who played freestyle hacky sack at lunchtime with Ray and other students. (Hacky sack is a type of ball-shaped beanbag where students, using only their feet, perform tricks while keeping the beanbag airborne for an extended period of time.) This student knew Ray had been learning Praying Mantis Kung Fu from a teacher who learned under Master Mark and had been in the same class as the infamous Bruce Lee. This student knew Ray had said he had nunchuks, ("Nunchuks" (nunchaku) are extremely popular among the street fighters.) Nunchaku is old martial art weapons consisting of two relatively short sticks, joined together by a cord or a metal chain. The average length of a stick is 11" - 16"; the cord's (chain's) length is about 6 "- 10". Nunchaku sticks are usually made of solid wood, hard plastic or metal (Self-defender)". Ray's nunchuks were made of metal and are definitely considered a dangerous weapon under zero tolerance, which is the absolute rejection of certain behaviors such as bringing weapons or drugs to school. Schools have adopted policies to impose serious penalties for even minor infractions of this law. Ray's Asian friend, who was upset Ray had not lied about what had happened at the art museum, told him he did not believe Ray had nunchuks and challenged him to bring them to school as proof.

Ray knew he could not carry his nunchuks around in school, but he wanted to prove to his Asian friend that he really did have them. He carefully smuggled them out of the house. Arriving at school, he carefully placed them on a jacket hook inside his locker. Ray's reasoning was that his new friend could not carry the nunchuks around in school because he knew that is what the school's law clearly states about weapons. He didn't understand someone couldn't just *see* the nunchuks.

Ray found out quickly that his new friend was not really his friend. After viewing the nunchuks in Ray's locker, the Asian student went to Ray's case manager and told her Ray had brought a weapon to school and gave her the location of where to find it. The case manager opened Ray's locker and took the nunchuks to the police officer at the school who in turn took the nunchuks to Assistant Principal Danube. Assistant Principal Danube summoned Ray into her office. Ray explained to Danube the sequence of events that led to his bringing the nunchuks to school. The principal immediately knew that the student who reported Ray was angry with him for telling the truth about who had damaged the painting frame in the art museum. She explained to Ray that the zero tolerance policy meant never bringing any weapon onto, around, or in a school, or anywhere else on school property. Ray hung his head with sadness and asked her if he was expelled. The assistant principal told him she would think about it. She took the situation to the head building principal who agreed with her not to prosecute Ray. They instead called me and let me know the "nunchuks" would come home in a paperbag carried by the bus driver.

After the first three weeks as a high school freshman, Ray felt very cool. He paired up with some very responsible senior mentors. Ray talked to his senior friends who explained what the unhappy Asian student had tried to do to Ray under the guise of friendship. They were very good mentors, able to answer any anxious questions he might have about life in high school.

Ray had a Kung Fu demonstration and had invited his high school teachers to attend. His math teacher came. Ray was very happy about it. When news of how well Ray had done in his Dojo's demonstration, Ray's case manager called an IEP meeting. At this meeting, the case manager tried to label Ray as a dangerous 6th degree Kung Fu professional who was now refusing to do his regular education work. I first explained there are no "degrees" in Kung Fu. The number six patches that the math teacher had described meant Ray had mastered six Kung Fu forms. I went on to describe how Kung Fu is *not* an aggressive martial art; it is a defensive martial art and would only be used if being attacked. Ray's case manager asked how I was going to explain Ray's refusal to do his regular education class work. I asked her exactly what she had asked of him. I learned she had asked him if he *wanted* to do the work ... to which he answered, no. I explained to the case manager that I was sure she could enter any classroom and ask the students if they *wanted* to begin their work and she would get the same answer, no! I explained she had given him a choice of working or not working and he gave the answer he thought he had a right to make. I illustrated to her that school was my children's job; they did not have a choice to do their work. Assistant Principal Danube shook her head in amazement and told the case manager to give students only choices of schoolwork or schoolwork!

After this meeting, I spoke to the case manager telling her Ray was a very easy and concrete person to work with. I needed her to understand the special education process because Moogie would be coming to the high school when Ray was a junior and he was not as easy to predict as Ray. The case manager turned to me and said Moogie could not come here because the principal did not want to turn this high school into a special education school. Of course, I requested another meeting in which she denied stating anything of the sort.

Musical Intelligence

When Ray was in his junior year of high school, Moogie was a freshman. They had both gotten a remarkable new case manager, Mrs. Curry. I thought Mrs. Curry was extraordinary. She actually listened to me and learned my sons' strengths and weaknesses. I wish I could clone her! To have a case manager that understands the different ways people learn was wonderful ... need I say more?

Ray was happy his brother Moogie was in high school with him and he told him so many times. The year was going great. Ray no longer needed to have a one-on-one para with him every minute. Ray was a well-liked student by all of his peers, teachers and the school staff, from the janitors to the paraprofessionals.

In the spring of Ray's junior year, he and the other students were ushered into the auditorium to hear a spring concert performed by the high school's Garage Band. Ray was mesmerized. After the band's performance, he walked up to the guitar teacher and told her he thought she and the band were amazing. He asked her how he could take her class and get into the Garage Band? He was told it would take three steps. First, he had to read music; second, he had to play an instrument; and third, he had to try out. Simple, unless you have never played an instrument before and have poor fine motor skills, both of which Ray had. The guitar teacher asked him what instrument he played. He told her he did not play an instrument but his mom had an acoustic guitar at home. The guitar teacher, amazed at what Ray was proposing to do with tryouts only two weeks away, gave Ray guitar tabs and all of the basic guitar chords B, E, A, D, G, C and F. I spoke with Ray when he arrived home and he excitedly told me what he wanted to do, asking if he could use the acoustic guitar and explaining why. He planned to master the chords in two days. I did not say anything to dampen his spirits; I understood he had to try. Mrs. Curry, my son's case manger, was terrified. She called me feeling both happy and scared for Ray. She told me how Ray had initiated and held a conversation with the guitar teacher and gathered all the necessary steps to attain his goal of being a musician. She was afraid of the big risk Ray had decided to take. What if he failed? I was overjoyed Mrs. Curry was concerned about Ray's welfare but we had to let him try. Friday, Saturday and Sunday nights after bedtime, I could hear Ray practicing his guitar chords.

Monday came and Ray came home after school feeling ecstatic. He had made it into the guitar class. He explained to me the guitar teacher was very happy that in two days he had mastered the basic chords and played the guitar with clarity. Mrs. Curry was likening to a proud mother hen and could not stop singing Ray's praises of how he had the courage to take a risk and had accomplished his goal. I was amazed he could master playing the guitar because of his poor fine motor skills but that was the incentive he needed to make him want to strengthen his fingers. In three weeks, he was finger picking complete songs. His guitar playing grew in a learning curve that was phenomenal to all of the school staff. He was playing Jimi Hendrix and Eric Clapton songs very well in less than three weeks. One of the janitors at the school, who played in a band, would go downstairs to the lunchroom to listen to Ray play his guitar and then join him. Ray found his calling, Rock 'n Roll!

Ray tried out and played the Star Spangled Banner for pep fest. He played at the wedding reception of the youth pastor at our church. It was a song the pastor's brother wrote the night before the wedding. How amazing! One of his Kung Fu instructors invited him to an "open mic" night at a local university where he joined other young musicians to play Rock 'n Roll. At his Kung Fu class, he found a bass player and another guitar player, who befriended him. He goes over to their houses to jam and spend the night. A perfect example of natural supports!

We experienced more natural supports during this time. The janitorial staff at the high school offered Ray a seasonal summertime job with the school district and the district hired him. His assignment was not at his own high school, however, but rather at a middle school on the south side of the district. Staff at this school did not want him, especially when they understood he was a person with developmental disabilities. Ray thought his disability was a blessing. He did not understand the passive-aggressive words and actions of the staff at this south school site. Staff behaviors included breaking wind every time Ray walked close by them or entered a room in which the others were already working. Other incidents occurred where Ray was given six packs of pop that belonged to the school and was told the pop was outdated so he could take them home with him for free. It wasn't true. Ray did not need to be labeled a thief simply because staff did not want to work with him. It wasn't long and another incident occurred. Realizing Ray's vulnerability, one of these co-workers announced that he wanted Ray to be his newborn child's Godfather and continued to explain what his responsibilities would be to a child whose father Ray had only known for two days. Ray was honored with this new responsibility. He came home and told his big sister, DeeDee, about his new title of Godfather. DeeDee explained to her brother that this young man was not a friend and only wanted to use Ray for his money. The janitorial staff at this school site had talked to me earlier and asked me why I had gotten Ray a *regular* job. Their analysis of where Ray should be working was with an enclave of disabled students who clean tables at nursing homes. After listening to their opinions of where Ray should be, I explained to them that I had nothing to do with his employment at the district.

One day Ray called and said the young man who had asked him to be the Godfather of his child was now walking by and breaking wind as Ray tried to work. I told Ray I was on my way to get him. I could hear the relief in his voice. I spoke with Ray. He informed me he did not think the janitors at this school liked him and maybe he should quit. I was relieved. I didn't want him to work in a place where the environment was not welcoming to him.

These passive-aggressive actions had gotten dangerous enough. I took Ray down to the district office and asked them not to put any negative remarks on his work record since I wanted him to resign early, before the summer was over. The head district janitor apologized for the behavior of the staff and asked Ray if he still wanted to work. Ray stated he did. As we sat in her office, she picked up the phone and called his old high school - the school where personnel had helped him fill out the online application for a janitorial job in the first place. Yes, they wanted him to work with them even now. Ray went over to the school and was accepted with open arms. These school janitors even had graduation presents for him in their cars and asked him to bring his acoustic guitar to play for them during lunchtime. Natural supports! What a difference in seeing a person as differently able and not just disabled!

The Helper

In tenth grade, Moogie had made friends with and without disabilities. Many public schools still offer special education students birthday parties in high school but Moogie told Mrs. Curry, his case manager, he did not want a party. Then one day I received a frantic call from Mrs. Curry explaining that Moogie had just left her office stating he wanted a birthday party *in* the autism resource room and he only wanted to invite students in the school with autism. Mrs. Curry was concerned I would assume someone talked him into having a party. I informed her I had no idea why Moogie made this request but it was his choice. After the party Mrs. Curry contacted me again in awe. She explained Moogie had overheard her and other staff talking about their concerns regarding the eating or non-eating habits of students with autism. Moogie marveled at how some of the other students had never tasted certain fruits and vegetables in their entire life so it was then he requested a healthy birthday party with bananas, strawberries, broccoli, cauliflower, carrots and carrot juice. When the party was over he gave her a list of foods that each student ate and which foods they enjoyed, instructing Mrs. Curry to get the food lists to the students' parents. Mrs. Curry asked Moogie how he knew these students would try new foods. He informed her he knew these fussy eaters would try the new foods because it was his birthday party and they liked him.

Moogie was earning an A+ in his biology class and he loved telling it to anyone who commented on his good work. Included in the report of his high grade, he would inform his listener he was only one of five students this teacher had ever given an A+ and there were no modifications to his work! The biology teacher asked Moogie to help write a curriculum for the class. He did. Moogie came up with a game where students could win large candy bars once a week by playing a game that taught biology vocabulary. It was quite successful.

We went to Dr. Bright's office during this year for a routine medication check up but also because Moogie still refused to go to school. School refusal is a serious legal issue. The district has no problem referring students to the county's child protection office for educational neglect and giving them the gift of a probation officer and/or a child protection worker. Dr. Bright wrote a letter to the school and gave me a copy for my records. In his letter, he stated that Moogie was in his care and we were working on this problem of school refusal. He asked the school not to act upon Moogie's missed school days. During this office visit, Moogie was given time to meet with Dr. Bright individually. When that time was over, Moogie came to invite me back to his session.

Dr. Bright happily told me Moogie was able to tell him the first time he felt fear and started panic attacks that had overwhelmed him ever since. Moogie told him the first time he did not feel safe was the day in first grade when he had held himself hostage and the school professionals wanted the police officer to hurt him. Dr. Bright said this was a tremendous step towards healing Moogie's fear. He was right!

In the summer after Moogie's tenth grade year, he asked me if he could try *not* taking any medication. I said yes, we could try. This was a major step for he was currently taking ADHD medication, panic attack medication , sleeping medication, and asthma medication. What the heck! It was summer time after all! DeeDee would be at home when I had to work. We decided to let him try.

Moogie has been medication free since that time. I called and let Dr. Bright know how Moogie was managing without his medication. The doctor was very pleased.

During the first two weeks of Moogie's junior year, he asked if he could ride the regular education bus. When I asked him why, he clearly explained to me how the students on the special education bus could not talk and he needed to practice conversation. He had watched the regular education buses pull up in front of the high school and observed there was lots of talking on those buses.

Moogie still takes regular education classes with one-on-one para support. He still has school phobia. Mrs. Curry left the school district and there is a new case manager that needs to learn not to talk down to Moogie. Life is always changing but Moogie is making leaps and gains in his learning … experiencing community living in the regular world.

Solving Whose Problem?

I had my youngest son, Gavin, evaluated the same time I had the rest of my children evaluated. He tested very high and was an eager learner. When he started elementary school, he was fine in kindergarten. First grade was where his problems began. The school district started training staff to use an intervention-solving model for students that might need special education services. Gavin had great grades. He was an outgoing, happy, very confident child who started coming home whining and complaining that he had no friends in school. I asked him what he did when he wanted to make friends. He told me the same things he did when we went to the park where he had no problem making friends and playing with children who were total strangers. I called the school about my concerns. His teacher stated Gavin had one girl as a friend.

Then Gavin came home one day and informed me his one friend had moved away and now he was alone in school. I tried encouraging him to keep trying to make friends even though his self esteem was falling like a person jumping from a plane without a working parachute. Although his grades were not suffering at this point, I enrolled Gavin into summer school, hoping he could make more friends.

One morning I was late taking my sons to daycare since Gavin had missed his bus by minutes and I had to drive him to summer school. The school was on the far side of a two block city lot with a community park located at the opposite end. As we drove to the backside of the school, Gavin pointed to a little boy and an even smaller girl exclaiming to me that this was a boy from his class and the other one was the boy's kindergarten sister. Since we were on the park end of the double block, I took this opportunity to ask Gavin if he would like to walk the rest of the way to school with his classmate and sister. Gavin's eyes lit up as he joyously agreed to this possibility. I stopped the car and Gavin jumped out. I pulled ahead and parked.

I watched as Gavin ran happily towards the two students; then suddenly stopped as though he had run full force into a brick wall. This sudden change was caused by the disturbing reaction from his peer. The young man held up his hands, blocking his younger sister behind him in a protective fashion. Screaming at the top of his lungs, he told Gavin to get away from them. The young boy went on to say that there must be something really wrong with Gavin since Gavin's desk was not sitting with the rest of the class.

What in the world was going on? Gavin came back to the car with his head hanging, chin touching his chest, first crying, then whining, saying he could not do anything right and no one liked him. This was the hopeless behavior in Gavin I was seeing at home. That day I learned it had come from the school.

This was the first time I brazenly walked into Gavin's school. Without signing in at the office, I walked straight to his classroom holding his hand. Gavin showed me his desk. It was in a corner away from all the other students in the class who assumed there was "something terribly wrong with Gavin". These students had come to undesirable conclusions about the safety of Gavin. They had no way of knowing the school staff was practicing their new intervention-solving problems, a model for students that *might* need special education services without really being evaluated for them.

I explained to both the teacher and the principal that I had never signed any papers nor was told anyone had concerns about my son's behavior. Upon my questioning them why they had put Gavin in isolation, the teacher explained to me she knew I was a "single mother"; she knew I already had two sons with disabilities; and she knew this was too much for any one person to handle. She further explained to me that grades were not the reason they decided to isolate Gavin since he was very smart. Her decision was based entirely on one incident of unwelcome behavior which occurred on a day at the beginning of first grade. The teacher explained to me how she told the class it was DEAR time, an acronym for Drop Everything And Read. Hearing this announcement, Gavin took off his shoes and came to the gathering circle of students on the floor. He immediately laid his head on the teacher's thigh, and closed his eyes, waiting for her to read the book. She deemed this behavior as sexually deviant.

The school keeps amazing me with their misunderstanding of children's behavior. I told the teacher and the principal that I was once an early childhood teacher and understand what DEAR means. We still use it in our home. I explained to them that when I say it is DEAR time at home, everyone comes to my room, takes off their shoes, and climbs up onto my canopy bed. When Gavin lies on his back, he puts his head on my thigh and closes his eyes as I begin to read our story book. I told them Gavin was an interactive child and had great self esteem. I explained to them he had just won first place in a community talent contest at the American Variety Theatre Company, hoping to give them a better and more well-rounded picture of Gavin's versatility and strengths.

Gavin was in regular education and he was experiencing the same misinterpretations of his behavior as my other sons had experienced in special education. I thought I had repeatedly explained the culture in our home to both the teacher and the principal to the point where they could now understand that the problem with Gavin's behavior in his classroom was because he did not understand the teacher's rules. They had agreed with me verbally and told me it all made sense to them ... Only for me to learn that all through second grade and half way through third grade, the school was still trying to solve a problem. Perhaps they were perfecting their model, *still* keeping Gavin isolated from the other students while waiting for some kind of explosive, deviant behavior that never occurred. Gavin's emotional behavior changed. He became very quiet and still did not think he was good enough at anything new he was trying to do when he was home. Nothing we tried at home or with our pastors and doctors seemed to help his self-esteem. Finally, I thought of the right question ("How big is the fly?") and asked Gavin if he was separated from his classmates again?   He hung his head and said yes, but not all of the time. Gavin told me how he had been sitting with everyone else until his classroom teacher talked to another teacher and then his desk was moved away from the other students. By the time I found out they were still isolating my son, his self esteem had tanked. He was now afraid of the dark; had no friends in school, only in our community; and began exhibiting the behaviors associated with ADHD (attention deficit hyperactivity disorder). I immediately went to the neighborhood school my daughter had attended throughout her elementary school days and enrolled him there. I met with the social worker, principal, and the teachers he would have for the rest of third grade. We put in place a time where Gavin could spend time with the student social worker who could help him feel a part of the school and not ostracized from it. The lead third grade teacher, Ms. Ginger, explained to me how Gavin's first action whenever he came into the classroom was to move his desk away from the other students. At first the co-teacher wanted to tell him he could not move school furniture around but Ms. Ginger stopped her. She wanted him to use his decision to separate himself from the others as a gauge that would let them know when and if he felt he was part of the class. At the end of his first week at this new school, Gavin moved his desk back to its original position. The rest of Gavin's school year went very well. Through the American Variety Theater Company, Gavin was chosen for an insurance commercial where the six foot seven inch director, John, told Gavin he was very tall for a third grader. John asked Gavin if other students in school teased him and Gavin answered yes … something I was not aware of. John went on to tell Gavin not to worry. Because of his height, the teasing would continue all the way through school until eighth grade. Then everyone would want to be his friend.

Gavin came home one day with a giant knot over his right eye. He explained to me that any time he went into the boys' restroom, older boys would tease him and hit him. I, of course, requested a meeting with Gavin's teacher, the assistant principal, and a social worker. Surprisingly, his teacher, Ms. Ginger, informed me that Gavin would have to take personal responsibility for his behavior that was causing the attacks on him from eighth grade boys. She requested the gym teacher attend this meeting because she had seen Gavin sitting in timeout in gym class almost every day when she came to pick up her class. To Ms. Ginger this was an indication to her that Gavin was having problems with these boys' on a daily basis. Never once did she believe Gavin when he told her he had not done anything to these boys; never once had she asked the gym teacher why Gavin was sitting in the timeout area during his class.

When the gym teacher arrived at the meeting, his story cleared up the matter of Gavin's behavior and his honesty about not doing anything that would cause these attacks on him. The gym teacher explained he had Gavin sitting in the timeout area, not because he had done anything wrong, but to protect him. It seems this gym class had eighth grade students that consistently picked on the younger third grade students in the class. The only thing the gym teacher could do to keep Gavin and other nonviolent students safe was to have them sit in timeout where they could be seen at all times. Ms. Ginger lowered her eyes and the assistant principal said they would try to get the older students out of the third grade gym class.

The rest of Gavin's third grade year was fine. At the beginning of his fourth grade year, we came into the school to look at his new classroom. As we walked toward his assigned classroom, his pace slowed and a look of unbelief came over his face. Exclaiming in a panic ridden voice, he stated he was now in the class with the teacher that screams at her students all the time. I asked how he knew it was all the time? Gavin explained any time he saw this teacher with her students she was screaming at them. Every time! I immediately went downstairs to try to get Gavin placed in the fourth grade classroom my daughter had been in at this school but it was over-filled. I told Gavin perhaps this teacher, Ms. Screamer, was having a bad year last year, and surely, he could understand what it was like to have a bad school year. Thus, Gavin started the school year off with uncertainty. Continually bullied at school, he would come home with bruises which no school staff could explain to me. He was an avid reader at home. Because of me, whenever he read in school, he would use animated voices for the different characters in the stories whenever the class read aloud. This was unwelcome behavior and Gavin would get in trouble from his teacher for doing this. I went to fall conferences where Ms. Screamer explained she did not allow that kind of reading in her classroom.

Then there was the day Gavin came home informing me I had lied to him and was not thinking about his health because we had movie night every Friday night at home. On our Friday movie night, permission was to given my children to stay up all night watching movies. I made that rule. Just the idea they could stay up all night was exciting enough for them even though they were never able to stay awake past their bedtime. They were always in bed asleep by eight thirty at night. As each student took turns sharing what they did together for family time, Gavin described our Friday night movie night. Ms. Screamer told him in front of the class, Friday night movie night was not a healthy thing to do and I must not care about his health. I was extremely perturbed at this teacher again! Why would anyone shame my child? Why would anyone shame any child? I went to school and explained to the social worker, then to Ms. Screamer about our family Friday movie night. I explained that I taught all of my children, starting with their strengths and using their interests, not their hobbies. I looked for anything that peaked their interests that we could use to investigate and cultivate together. Then I asked Ms. Screamer for her class's curriculum mapping so I could use it to cultivate interest for my son. She stated she would make a copy for me but she never did.

In our community, we happened to run into two of Gavin's classmates and their parents at the grocery store. I asked the parent for her opinion of Ms. Screamer. She knew Ms. Screamer was very loud and stern with children. She had requested a class change for her daughter from Ms. Screamer's room to another classroom and the principal had it done. She told me she had heard stories from her children of how negatively Ms. Screamer treated Gavin. Her daughter spoke up and informed me that Ms. Screamer did not like Gavin and none of the students knew why she picked Gavin out everyday. I wondered if Ms. Screamer was afraid of my child or if she was retaliating because I was involved with his learning.

During the pre-Christmas break, or winter holiday break as the school named it, Gavin showed excitement again about attending school. He had taken his allowance and spent it all at the dollar store to get his friends in his class, love gifts. Love gifts are what we called Christmas gifts at home. The night before this special day for him, Gavin had excitedly gotten ready for the holiday party they were having in his classroom. He left for school the next day with his love gifts.

Needless to say, I was stunned when I received a call that day from a neighbor woman who found Gavin stumbling down our block barely breathing in the frigid weather. She brought him into her home and had him use his inhaler. I came home from work, took him home, and put him on the nebulizer. I asked Gavin what in the world would make him leave his school in weather he knew was dangerous for his health, then walk through a dangerous neighborhood with level three sexual perpetrators in order to come home when he did not even have a key to get into the house. He explained how Ms. Screamer told the class to read a short story she had assigned and then to write a summary about it. The students needed to write down their summary of the beginning, the middle and the end of the story. Ms. Screamer explained to the class that, after everyone had turned in their story, they would go to the restroom and then come back for the holiday celebration. Excitedly, Gavin told me he wrote on his paper the beginning followed with an explanation of what he remembered had happened in the story; then he wrote the middle followed by his explanation of that; and last he wrote the end and what he thought had transpired there. He said when he took his paper up to Ms. Screamer, she looked at it and yelled at him in front of the whole class as he was returning to his seat, saying his paper was a joke and not acceptable.

Punishment for being an excited child with visions of a holiday party in his eyes, he was made to sit out in the hallway writing two hundred sentences saying," I will not take short cuts when doing the work my teacher gives me." Gavin was devastated as he watched the class go to the restroom, then return to their classroom to begin their celebration of the holidays. Heartbroken, Gavin went to his locker, put on his coat and left. The school staff said happy holidays to him as he left the building. Crying he walked home in sub-freezing weather, the sobbing and frigid temperatures triggered his asthma. If our neighbor had not been outside shoveling, he could have died. After DeeDee, now 19 years old, arrived home, I called the school. They did not know Gavin was gone. I proceeded to the school for a meeting with the head principal. As I spoke to him about the continuing problems with Gavin's teacher such as failing him on anything that was not to her taste, the principal continually reassured me how all of his teachers were caring people. He assured me his teachers would not just let a student fail in their classes because there were processes in place that were there to assist students who were having problems. I asked for an administrative transfer for Gavin to a Montessori school for the rest of the school year. The principal apologized about the fact Gavin was able to walk out of the school without the knowledge of any adult staff. Then he proceeded to inform me there were many parents trying to get their children into that particular Montessori school I had requested and, unfortunately, there was a waiting list. He asked me to give the teacher another chance. He would talk with her directly.

When I came to school on a Friday morning for winter conferences, I was met with rudeness from Ms. Screamer, who stated Gavin could not read very well. I begged to differ. He was reading tenth grade books with understanding and his evaluations I had done disproved what she was stating. This teacher did not know I had had independent evaluations done for all of my children. I asked her to give me her curriculum mapping so I could supplement Gavin's work at home. With that she threw the reading list and his work, all bearing an "F" grade, across the table at me and said, "Have at it girl friend!" Luckily, I am not a volatile type of person. Instead of wasting time screaming at her, I knew I had to get my son away from such a toxic individual. I left this meeting with Ms. Screamer and went downstairs to talk to the head principal. When I laid Gavin's report card of all "F's" down on his desk, without saying a word, he immediately picked up his phone and called the principal at the Montessori school who agreed to let Gavin start there on Monday.

Gavin had a male teacher, Mr. Z, at the Montessori school. In one day he made friends. In fourth, fifth and sixth grade, Gavin was finally having great learning experiences in public school. The time it took for us to find a school that understood children's strengths, cost Gavin to miss the beginning foundations of education and caused a gap in his math learning. I had, however, found a school where teachers built on the strengths of children and he would not have a gap in his motivation. These teachers understood all people are unique and not everyone is a linguistic and logical learner. Not being like everyone else was okay in this place!

Researchers have identified a gap showing that African-American children fall behind their Euro-American peers. I wonder if there is any research showing in which grades that happens. I do not remember such a gap when I attended school. Is it occurring in third and fourth grades? If students and parents have to go through what we, as a family, have had to work through, it is no wonder they can form distrust or a dislike for public schools.

Money

My daughter, DeeDee, took dance and acting classes. She had a network of friends at the American Variety Theatre Company. She can dance like an angel. It is one of her purposes here on earth; it is one of her gifts from God. I remember the first time she showed me a dance she had choreographed. It was very professional and she was only 12 years old at the time. She encouraged Moogie to join the acting and tap dancing classes. He did and he enjoyed it. Ray would go to the theatre but he would only watch.

DeeDee had great elementary and middle school teachers who engaged both the students and the parents. I remember in 1998 there were grant monies for high-risk students. There began a big undercurrent of talk about how the district was teaching, using tracks "high" and "low". I remember signing a paper stating I did not want my daughter to become part of a survey done by the local university that would prove how "high risk" she and other students in single parent homes actually were. Why should she take the university's survey? I taught my children they can over come all odds. I showed them how, all through history, there have been single parents in the African-American communities raising gifted and contributing citizens. Starting on the slave plantations, after a couple jumped the broom and became a married couple, there was no guarantee family units would not be broken apart by their owners who treated them like property, not like human beings. In North America slave families who were formed from Africa, were broken apart and sold as individuals. In the Caribbean Islands, African slaves could marry and, if their owners sold them, it was as a family unit.

Despite the unstable foundation of the African-American family unit, when we each choose to be included individuals and embrace our heritage, we continue to raise brilliant persons who think about the betterment of the whole community. When African-Americans as individuals decide to integrate, we either loose the caring and village mentality of raising all of our children as one or we become the black /white-man person who only thinks of self and self-advancement.

Here are some of the contributions African-American slaves and single-parented families have imparted to this country.

- Hudson, G.H. Garrett Augustus Morgan: Big Chief Mason, ingenious American.

- Jenkins, E.S. Ernest E. Just, cell physiologist.

- Ryder, E.C. George Washington Carver, agricultural scientist.

- Jackson, W.S. Benjamin Banneker, Black astronomer.

- Jenkins, E.S. Percy L. Julian, soybean chemist.

- Jackson, W.S. Granville T. Woods, railway communications wizard.

- Hudson, G.H. Charles Richard Drew, blood plasma pioneer.

- Hudson, G.H. Charles Henry Turner, scientist, teacher, author, humanitarian.

- Hudson, G.H. Matthew A. Henson, famous explorer.

- Jenkins, E.S. Leon Roddy, spider man.

- Ryder, E.C. Elijah McCoy, inventor.

- Ryder, E.C. Daniel Hale Williams, pioneer heart surgeon.

(African Americans 2006)

Peanut butter, the stop light, the shoe machine, the ironing board, the indoor toilet, jazz, rock 'n roll, literature and much more.

After explaining our African-American history to DeeDee and signing the paper stating I did not want her to participate, I found out later that the principal of her middle school had threatened students with suspensions if they did not fill out the survey. I know it is true that children, who are "high risk" students, bring money into the district but whatever happened to the rights of parents, even single parents?

Searching for answers about the processes in the school district, I found some students who were not considered worth the time and effort to teach and were quickly placed in a "low track" of learning. My question is this: if one does not believe *all* can learn, why would one want to become an educator?

I have met and spoken with too many very good teachers who have left a district, not because of excess paper work, but because of rules that do not allow them to teach in a variety of ways. A teacher cannot step outside of the rules if they want to continue to teach. When I say "step outside", I am talking about going the extra mile to help a child learn. Some districts have had far too many teachers who have abused students emotionally and/or physically. How can this happen? When a professional does not do their job, for whatever reason, the outcome is never good. When a professional cannot accept they made a mistake and take responsibility for their mistake, what are they modeling for the children they are teaching?

I read about a young African-American male student who was in middle school. He was an average student, not in special education, who was shamed by a professional. A teacher made him crawl down a student-filled hallway. She later stated it was a joke; she just wanted him to deliver an item to give her. This story was on the front page of the local newspaper. How many stories like this have not made the newspapers? The damage to this young African-American male's self-esteem is not acceptable. It makes me think of all children who think of school as a safe place. Teachers, who want to stay after school to help students, say they are not allowed to do so in some school districts. Moreover, by law, we, as parents, must send our children into this Russian roulette hostile/healthy environment to learn. There was an African-American community woman who pulled her children out of the public schools to home school them. She asked all parents to boycott the district because they were purposely under-educating our children. There was no boycott. Most parents were not given the information with which she was trying to distribute to inform others.

Accountability For All Students and Teachers

Years later the federal government passed, No Child Left Behind (nclb), for our nation's public schools. Gavin was in seventh grade. The middle school he attended was one of three middle schools in our district. It was a major change from the Montessori school. Not one educator wondered why Gavin lost his motivation to learn. He would learn and research many things at home and with his friends in the community; in school he would just sit and wait for the day to end. I found out he was failing his classes when I called the school to find out why he had no homework. I requested a meeting at which the educators stated Gavin sat in class and did nothing for the first three weeks. No one contacted me by home phone, email or cell phone. One teacher showed me papers where my telephone number and email address were transcribed incorrectly. Amazing! They could have mailed a letter through the post office that I would have received within those three weeks!

In writing, I requested a 504 plan, which included extended time for Gavin's assignments to be given to the teachers. After meeting with the principal and teachers, the 504 plan has been totally ignored. I would receive emails from two of the teachers. I would get promises from them of work to be sent home, which would never be sent until one or two days 'til the end of the quarter.

Safe Learning Environment

How do our children attend schools to learn when they are not safe? When I came to pick Gavin up from school, there had been a fight in the room where students must go if their grades are not good enough to attend the school's dance. As we were leaving, Gavin pointed out to me the boy in the assistant principal's office who had pulled a knife on another student in this classroom for children with bad grades. We left quickly to get out of the way. I explained to my son that the law states this young man would not be in school the following Monday … only to receive an accusing phone call from Gavin at school telling me the knife-wielding student was indeed at school on Monday! I immediately called the principal and was put in touch with one of the police liaison officers who told me the teacher had never said anything about a knife. Students had both seen and made loud comments about the knife in front of the teacher who was there breaking up the fight and calling for help. This uncovering of such a dangerous incident did not help Gavin who was now pitted against a teacher with adult friends, and other teachers as well who did not like me. Now, because he had told me the truth, he would not get any help the rest of the year. Why, you may ask? As I stated earlier, the incident of the knife was never reported by the teacher. This could have cost her her job.

LSB

Understanding the concrete thinking of my children has been an interesting and wonderful journey. Persons who learn on the autism spectrum have certain sensory issues with fabric; they sometimes only accept certain types of material. When Moogie was a junior in high school, he preferred loose cotton, hospital scrub-like clothing and very large cotton T-shirts. He liked the feel of satin material. All of this to introduce to you a story I consider funny about LSB ...

One holiday season I received a silk lingerie set with pajamas and robe with laced sleeves. Moogie saw my set and became excited about the material, asking me if he could try on the robe. I said, sure. Just as he was about to put his right arm into the sleeve of robe, Gavin said in a stern voice for Moogie to stop moving. He quietly walked over to Moogie and whispered something in his ear. Moogie slowly removed his arm from the sleeve and folded it as if it was contaminated. He carefully laid it next to me. Taking a giant step backwards, Moogie asked me if the robe was lingerie? I answered yes, it was. Then Moogie announced to me if he had put my robe on he could have become an LSB. When I asked him what an LSB was, he informed me it meant he could have become a "Lingerie Slave Boy". It was very hard for me not to burst into laughter. Another new Moogie acronym was born!

Fix the disabled

Moogie did not want to attend school anymore. He asked to get his diploma on line; he asked to attend school part time. He does not want to go into a school environment that does not listen to what he is telling them about his unique needs. This is not good. I was informed by one of the school professionals that school could "make" him go to school by putting him in the juvenile justice system and giving him a probation officer because of truancy. This would not be a positive motivator for my son. I would loose my son. Why? He would not understand their demands and it would ruin him. It would destroy our family. How many students have probation officers because their school environment is hostile to their unique needs? "In addition to suffering higher rates of suspension, students, especially African-Americans, are increasingly finding themselves referred to juvenile court for minor infractions at school. (zero tolerance)". This is happening across our nation. Sadly, our school district is no different.

We, as a nation, are criminalizing school children. Not all children are linguistic and logical learners. Not all students can sit in a classroom and listen to lectures as though they are in a college setting. Does this make them abhorrent or does it just show there are all kinds of people who learn in all kinds of different ways?

When they enter a classroom, do we expect children to know instantly each teacher's teaching philosophy? - a teaching philosophy that took each professional teacher an entire semester or more to begin understanding themselves!

How Big is the Fly?

I attended an east coast Ivy League school symposium on civil rights and learned about over-identifying minority children in special education. One of the many lessons I acquired was stated by a guest professor who said that the only way to fix special education was to fix regular education. Communication must occur between parents and educators in a straight forward fashion in order for our educational system to improve and grow to the level it should be. Educators, who are public servants, need to keep their passion for teaching while understanding they are human beings who are capable of making mistakes ... and we understand, mistakes will *always* happen. Believe me, honest mistakes are and will be made because there is no manual that comes with each individual child or situation.

Police should never be posted inside a public school because they work from a totally different set of rules. Children are not looked upon as children in the eyes of the police. Police are not trained to be educators; they are keepers of the law. If the law/rule is broken, it is the police liaison's job to arrest, write a ticket, and haul a person away in handcuffs. If educators are afraid of the students they are teaching, they should not be in that setting. When we criminalize children for their natural childlike behavior, behavior everyone has seen in public schools growing up, we end up with a broken society. Not allowing the natural growth of children and allowing them to *be* children ... allowing them to make child mistakes ... is like pulling a butterfly out of its cocoon as it is trying to grow and form its wings to fly. We have to learn teamwork as we educate our children. We have to allow teachers to teach just as we have to allow children to be children. Teachers should not be driven by someone in a union somewhere, telling them when they can teach, whom they can teach, and how they can teach the district's curriculum.

Bonnie Jean Smith

I believe parents should have the right to know the teaching philosophy of each teacher. This, in turn, would allow parents to help their children understand that style of teaching being used to educate them. Moreover, this process would make sure there is at least a chance for a meeting of the minds between teaching and learning styles. Sometimes personalities and learning/teaching styles clash, too. It takes all kinds of people to make this world balanced. Each of us can speak for ourselves; we do not need a lot of research to tell us what does not work for us. Every day we work to be independent, productive, self-determined, and included citizens in our schools, neighborhoods, communities, cities, states and nation. I continue to learn, enjoy and marvel at children who strive at becoming their best and reaching their dreams.

When it comes to unwelcome behavior by anyone, I have learned through my journey with all my children to not just ask questions but to search for the right question to ask them, such as "How Big is the Fly?"

References

African-Americans: November 26, 2006-
https://webfiles.uci.edu/mcbrown/display/inventors_bibliography.
html

(c b) Columbine high school:
www.cnn.com/SPECIALS/2000/columbine.cd/frameset.exclude.
html

Deborah Sampson: (b. 17 Dec 1760 d. 29 Apr 1827-
http://www.rootsweb.com/~nwa/sampson.html

Partners (2007). www.mnddc.org

Self Defender: October 20, 2006-
http://www.self-defender.net/weapons/nunchuks.htm

Walt Disney Movie: (1964) *Mary Poppins*

Wikipedia: http://en.wikipedia.org/wiki/Communication

(nclb) No Child Left Behind: www.ed.gov/nclb/landing.jhtml

Urban Dictionary: 2007-
http://www.urbandictionary.com/define.php?term=hustler

(1998) Jerry Springer Show-
www.cnn.com/SHOWBIZ/TV/9806/29/kitman.springer/index.
html?eref=sitesearch

Zero tolerance: February 20, 2003-
http://www.buildingblocksforyouth.org/kentucky/ky_local_release.html

About the Author

Bonnie Jean Smith is an American author, advocate, mentor and parent. Ms. Smith's family moved frequently due to her father being a member of the US military; living in diverse locales such as: France, Michigan, and Colorado. Upon graduating high school, she attended Wichita State University (1971-1974), majoring in Education. Ms. Smith's professional background and resume are quite extensive. She is the 1986 Honor Graduate of the US Army Patient Administrations School, a former member of Minnesota Governor's Council on Developmental Disabilities (1998–2006), served as a National Monitoring and Technical Review Team member for the Federal Administration on Developmental Disabilities (current), serves as a State of Minnesota Council for Quality Evaluator (1999 - 2007), attended Harvard University Civil Rights Symposiums (2000-2003) and Harvard University Multiple Intelligences (2003).

Her distinguished career and training also chronicle numerous situations over the past thirty years she has advocated and coordinated implementation of legal, medical, educational and other social service systems on behalf of children and families. She has worked extensively developing programs and solutions for Woman's Advocate, Inc. (first battered women's shelter in the nation). As Supervisor of Early Learning Center (Phillips Community Initiatives for Children - Minneapolis, Minnesota), Smith supervised staff and volunteers; evaluated, improved and implemented childcare programming needs; provided advocacy for children and parents with special needs. Working currently as a Parent Advocate Trainer, she teaches parents where they are and how to navigate the Special Education processes.

Her first published book, "How Big is the Fly" (ISBN 9781434305220, AuthorHouse™), chronicles a parent who has learned to develop practical and useful problem solving capabilities based on the foundation that "asking the right questions" while working with children in crisis situations, will always yield positive results. Over the years, Ms. Smith has developed a wealth of extensive knowledge to realize methods and implement workable strategies that relate to empowering other parents to better advocate for themselves and their families.